Soaring with Eagles, Flying with Turkeys?

An inspirational journey of travel and adventure, helping others across the world

Phil Beswick

HOT POT PUBLISHING

Published by Hotpot Publishing
All rights reserved.
ISBN: 978-0-9575400-0-2

Dedication

This book is dedicated to my family, parents Kenneth and Sylvia, my brother Andy and my niece and nephew, Ella and Jack.
Also for my grandparents Wilfrid & Edna Beswick, Fred and Nora Royle and my Aunt Christine and Uncle Jeffrey - all now on the higher side of life.

I would also like to thank all my friends in Bury, Harrogate and from all around the world for some truly amazing times and memories over the years.

Love and light to you all.

Contents

Acknowledgments   1

Foreword   2

1   Sometimes Goodbye is a Second Chance   7

2   Feed the Need, Not the Greed   14

3   Running Against the Tide   26

4   A Stumble at the First Hurdle   38

5   Mad Dog and an Englishman   53

6   Whoa, Whoa, Whoa, Sweet Child O'Mine   66

7   Buckets, Bad Guts and a New Year   86

8   Beauty and the Beast   97

9   This is Gonna Hurt!   108

10 The Adventures of the Red Shed   120

11 Treasure Island   150

12 The Return of the Bum Gun   163

13 Crossing Borders   173

14 The Way of St. James   190

15 I Did it My Way   214

Acknowledgments

I would like to thank the following people for their help, support and guidance in producing this book:

Robert Weston for all his patience, diligence, help and support in editing my book. robertwestonlee@yahoo.com

Leanne Mansfield for turning my ideas and drawings into the wonderful final cover artwork. www.leannemansfield.co.uk

Mark Walling for the back cover photograph. mwalling@sky.com

To all fellow travellers around the globe and anyone else I met during the writing of this book; it was a pleasure to meet each and every one of you and to share our wonderful experiences of life together.

For the following artistes for providing strength, comfort, inspiration and motivation with their music and lyrics throughout the journey:- Iron Maiden, Europe, Dan Reed, Chris Cornell, Metallica, Slash, Journey, Thunder, Scorpions and far too many others to name. Rock 'n f%^!*' roll!

For all my travel and adventure, motivational coaching and spiritual inspiration, my thanks goes to Charley Boorman and Ewan McGregor, Bill Bryson, Richard Branson, Robin Sharma, the medium Gordon Smith and so many others for keeping me focused and grounded through their amazing books. I would also like to thank Bury Football Club for the constant entertainment, ups and downs over the last 35 or so years as a loyal supporter. Up The Shakers!

And finally, to those who passed into spirit as this book was written. Love and light.

Phil x

Foreword

Whether we like it or not, we live in a time where the 'celebrity culture' appears to be a part of everyday life. It has got so out of hand that now there are even those who are famous for not being famous. The media fawn over this plethora of nobodies, force feeding us every minute detail of their lives as though they are important, as though hearing about their lives will enrich ours. If celebrity X has had a vagazzle or celebrity Y is dating celebrity Z, it is plastered all over the newspapers' front pages as though it is the news story of the decade.

Whilst all this undeserved, sycophantic idol worship is happening, in the real world, ordinary people are doing truly extraordinary things – things that really matter – without ever hitting the front page. Phil Beswick is one of those people.

Less than two years ago he would have appeared to be a stereotypical ordinary guy. With a career in the prison service, a wife, mortgage and foreign holidays, there was nothing about his life that would have made him stand out from the crowd. If fate hadn't stepped in, perhaps his life would have continued down that same route until the day retirement beckoned. We'll never know, because fate did step in, emotionally trampling him underfoot in the process.

What would you do if your world fell apart? Call the Samaritans? Throw yourself into your work? Hit the bottle? Pick up what pieces you can and muddle through in much the same way as before in a permanent state of unhappiness? Give up and buy a one-way ticket to Beachy Head? Not Phil - apart from a short-term relationship with the aforementioned bottle - he did something completely different.

As an unwilling victim of circumstance, his planned holiday to New Zealand had to be cancelled. So what was he to do with time he had booked off work? He could have resumed his affair with the vodka bottle, staying at home feeling sorry for himself. He didn't. Instead he spent three weeks in Nepal as a volunteer at a children's orphanage. That experience turned out to be a catalyst for change. Touched by the plight of the Nepalese children, he returned to England a changed man. This experience led to him re-evaluating his life, considering what was important and what was not - and that re-evaluation led to some truly momentous decisions.

So it was that, in September 2011, Phil set out on an incredible journey of discovery, visiting far flung parts of the world. Sure, many young people strap a rucksack to their backs and set off into the blue yonder for a thrill seeking, hedonistic 'gap year.' What, you may ask, makes Phil Beswick's journey any different? Simple, his was not a self-gratifying pursuit of personal pleasure; he set out to bring joy into the lives of other people, rather than his own. That's not to say he didn't have fun along the way – of course he did - but there were times too when the difficulties he encountered were anything but fun.

'Soaring with Eagles, Flying with Turkeys?' is his account of that journey. Although it could be described as a tale of travel and adventure, in the same vain as those undertaken by Michael Palin, Charlie Boorman and Ewan McGregor, it is so much more than that. The wonderful, exotic places he visited are the backdrop to his story rather than the star of the show. Phil was not setting out to discover the world; he was trying to discover his place in it. I suppose you could say he was looking for answers even though, when he set out on his journey, he didn't really know what the question was. He wasn't looking for the meaning of life; he was looking to give his life meaning.

Being on his own, there was no one there to share his thoughts and feelings with, no one to lean on for support when he needed it, no one to share the joy. He had no safety net either, if it all went wrong, there was no coming back; there was nothing to come back to - he'd rented his house and given almost all his belongings away. So he had no choice; he had to rely on his inner strength and resilience to overcome the many hurdles put in his way – and move on. How scary must that have been?

His story is inspiring because it isn't just about him; it's about you and me as well. It demonstrates what the human spirit can overcome – if we really want it to; it highlights what we are all capable of if we are willing to make changes, take on challenges and choose to do what we want to do rather than what others expect us to.

Phil is indeed an extraordinary guy, one of a kind. He puts any celebrity to shame. There was no ulterior motive behind his journey, no lucrative TV or book deal, no fat pay cheque, no bottomless budget - indeed no funding other than what came from his own pocket. He wasn't looking to resurrect his career or raise his profile; he was looking to resurrect his life and raise his expectations of it.

I've never met Phil. I only know him, as you now will, through the pages of this book. I hope you find his story as inspiring as I did. Join him now on his journey – and enjoy it.

Robert Weston
December 2012

''What you earn is how you make a living; what you give is how you make a life.''

Anon

''If you don't have a go, you'll never know''

Wilfrid Beswick

"You may be disappointed if you fail,
But you are doomed if you do not try"

Brigitte Trinkle

1

Sometimes Goodbye is a Second Chance

Glancing around at the boxes piled around the living room, a strange sense of déjà vu washed over me. I sat on one of the boxes and thought about how I had been in exactly the same position only two years earlier. Back then we had just moved into our nice three bedroomed, semi-detached house in a leafy suburb of Harrogate, North Yorkshire, seizing the opportunity of a recession hit, deflated housing market, giving us the chance to start and build up from there. We'd sold the old house in record time and this one had been too good an opportunity to miss.

Now, only a short time later, I was moving out. It wasn't that I really wanted to - but I had to. For some time I had needed to do something. I hadn't known quite what, but I had to make changes in my life, and this time I had actually done it.

For the next twelve months at least, I wouldn't have a choice in the matter. I'd rented out our marital home, taken a career break after sixteen years in the same career and was about to step away from everything that was familiar and safe to throw myself into a year of planned exile, pushing myself in a totally different direction to see what would happen.

And the reason for this apparent act of madness?

My wife had left me nine months earlier.

***

We all have key dates that we remember fondly, ones that signify something, forever to be permanently engrained in our memories and consciousness. For me, Saturday 18th July 2009 is one date that will forever stay etched on my mind. It was the date of my marriage.

I'd always had a problem with commitment. When in my thirties I did wonder whether I would ever get married. Would I ever meet someone that warranted me committing to them for the rest of my life? That question was answered when I met a wonderful girl called Gemma some two and a half years earlier. The day finally came when I succumbed, agreeing to say 'I do' to the woman who wanted to become my wife. To me she was the person I had grown to cherish most - and I loved her dearly.

Since I'd proposed to her, we spent the next twelve months, like most couples do, working hard and saving what we could. We also set about organizing and planning our wedding. We neither wanted nor needed anything flash or fancy; a small, intimate 'do' at a local hotel with our families and friends present suited our needs perfectly. We were more interested in throwing our money at a good honeymoon and not putting ourselves in the position of starting our married life in debt.

In the week before our wedding I had to attend a family funeral and, with the impending house move around a month overdue, after endless communication breakdowns with the solicitors, we had to pack up the old house and move into the new one only two days before married life began. Stressful? Yes, definitely. But somehow, we managed to get through it. I certainly thought that, with the week we'd both had, surely we could cope with anything the future might throw at us.

At 38, I was thirteen years older than my wife. Neither of us had been married before, but nonetheless had brought lots of life experiences to the table - which helped lessen the fact that there was a sizeable, but manageable, age gap. Friends and family had said we were a wonderful couple, perfect for each other. No one could see anything but a long and happy marriage - and children too.

The honeymoon was every bit as good as we hoped it would be, two and a half weeks of five-star luxury in Cancun, Mexico, being pampered and chilling out, enjoying diving and tours – a great start to married life.

When we returned, we began sowing the seeds of our future together. The next few months were great, decorating and refurnishing our new 'forever home,' which even had a log burning stove in the living room, providing endless hours of entertainment. How I loved to play hunter-gatherer, foraging for logs in the woods beyond our home and enjoying regular walks with our pet dog. Life was perfect. We had a good set of friends on both sides, family who visited regularly and great nights out. We decided to plan a family as soon as possible, once we had returned from New Zealand, a trip we had both wanted to take for a long time and a country I'd longed to visit. This was to be our goal for January 2011.

Even from the start of our married life there had been some issues. We both thought these were just teething problems and that they would sort themselves out in due course. Petty arguing over trivial things had started and, like many other couples, we had money issues - despite both of us holding full time jobs. Every penny had to be accounted for. We could still afford to have treats, days out and nice meals in restaurants every now and again, but we had to account for all our outgoings and sometimes it caused a rift between us. Towards the end of October 2010, things seemed to have reached a point where, whatever I said or did, it was never right. There was so much tension in the air, I felt like I was walking on egg shells all the time. Still, this was supposed to happen, wasn't it?

Sunday 21st November 2010 is another of those dates I can never forget. That day began just like any normal day in our household. We had been planning our trip to New Zealand over the past six months and were due to go only five weeks later. We'd laughed and joked about travelling around in a camper van, visiting relatives and friends. We were just gearing ourselves up for a quiet Christmas first. Having worked a lot of overtime over the past twelve months, I hadn't had much spare time, the focus being on saving what we could for this soon to be wonderful time away together.

I just wasn't prepared for the bombshell Gemma was about to drop. When we had said our vows, how could I possibly have foreseen that less than eighteen months later, just after finishing off a lovely lamb shank dinner, I would hear these words?

"I want to go; I'm not happy; I'm leaving you."

They hit me like a 10 ton battering ram; I don't think it sank in for the first two days. I couldn't believe it, how could this have been the answer? We knew things were difficult at times, but surely not this – not now.

"Why, what have I done wrong?" I asked her. "Please, let's sit down and talk. Go to your friend's house and we can chat tomorrow."

There was no reply. She had already said what must have been one of the hardest things for her to say.

Suddenly, without warning, came the uncontrollable crying and pain. I had never in all my life felt so vulnerable, so helpless. Here I was, a grown man, reduced to a quivering, emotional wreck in a matter of minutes.

Even though I'd stopped smoking some twelve months earlier, it didn't seem to matter anymore. Vodka and cigarettes became my companion that night, both a welcome comfort on that cold, bleak November evening. After she had walked out, in disbelief I sat by the back door in constant tears. Biscuit, our beautiful little Jack Russell dog lay in my arms giving me loving licks to my face, unaware that the two people who loved her the most and had given her a new home, had now separated. Nor did she know that looking after her would be so much harder from now on.

For two days I couldn't face anything. I wanted my wife back. I had never loved anyone like I loved her. My heart felt like it had been ripped from my chest, leaving a crater of nothingness. I no longer felt complete, a huge void had suddenly appeared and it hurt so much.

When I couldn't bear it any longer, I went to my parent's house in Bury, Lancashire. Neither parent could feel my pain but, with the same thing happening to my brother almost two years previously, they understood, which helped my turmoil. I had to ring work to tell them I couldn't come in. No way could I face that. In sixteen years unblemished service I had never had a sick day, but that day was different. Being a manager in the Civil Service, I held a responsible position that required a high degree of professionalism. That was impossible.

When I returned home, my wife had also returned - but now separate bedrooms became the salvation. We barely talked; it was too difficult, yet the pain etched into both of our faces was so evident. After a couple of weeks trying to live in the same house, things were heading nowhere. This couldn't carry on. If we were to be able to sort this out in any way, one of us would have to move out, giving us both time and space. Gemma didn't want to leave but, as she had family in the area, it seemed the most logical decision to make.

The first major decision that had to be acted upon came up within that first week. We had to decide whether or not to cancel our trip to New Zealand. After telling me there was no way she could go, suggestions that she offered like 'sell the tickets on eBay' or 'give the ticket to your mate in Vietnam' became almost laughable. Nonetheless, I had to cancel our dream trip. No doubt any refunds given would have to be redistributed into the pockets of solicitors, gleefully rubbing their hands together at the prospect of financially crippling yet another cruel victim of circumstances.

***

"I'm going to write a book," I told two of my closest friends as the car sped up the motorway heading for the Lake District.

"I've no idea what it will be about; I just know I have to do it."

Quite where this had come from, even I didn't know. I was a practical man, an artist, a carpenter; I was a doer, not a writer. I'd never written anything other than various work reports or job applications but, for some unknown reason, I unleashed that rather bold statement. I had no idea how it would come about, but I knew I had to do it.

I had also told them that I'd been quiet on the way to our yearly outing as my wife had left me five days earlier and I was somewhat still in a state of shock.

I don't know which of these two revelations surprised them the most. They both looked at each other, squirming awkwardly in the front seats, not quite knowing what to say to make things better for me.

During that weekend, uneasy glances from some of my other friends told me that they knew something was wrong; you can't be friends with people for up to 40 years without them being able to pick up on signs and moods. When I also told them about the split, I remember them saying 'yes, I know' or 'it was obvious.' I suppose that would be what 'coming out' might feel like - building up the courage to speak out, trying to find the right words - only to find out that everybody knew anyway. Still, the support was superb and, wrapped in an amazing blanket of love and support; I gained a lot of strength from my friends during that weekend. It even allowed me to start thinking of the future. Quite what that would entail, God only knew at this stage but at least I was opening my mind to it.

The next six weeks followed in a way to be expected following any split - difficult. Christmas now became an insignificant date in the future instead of the quiet, blissful one planned, looking forward to touring around New Zealand. With the trip cancelled, I just wanted to bury my head in the sand and forget about the position I'd found myself in. But one thought I did have was what was I going to do with the five weeks time off I had through January and February? I certainly didn't want to give it up, but I definitely didn't want to do nothing. As I sat on the settee one day, dog on my lap, I started to think about it.

2
Feed the Need, Not the Greed

I decided I needed to do something different about the position I was in. With our planned trip to New Zealand cancelled and over a month off work, I was wondering just what I could do with my time. One day in early December, sitting alone in the house, an idea suddenly hit me. I should go volunteering abroad. So, there I was, early January 2011, heading off to Nepal.

Having previously been a volunteer leader on working holidays with the National Trust and, having travelled alone to Europe and Australia before, the thought of being alone in a strange country for a couple of weeks didn't seem such a bad idea. I just knew that I had to do something positive and constructive with the month off work.

A couple of hours on the internet and my idea had started to take shape. I found an opportunity to go to Nepal as a volunteer in an orphanage with Original Volunteers, a company who specialise in giving people the chance to become involved in something they generally would not have the chance to. So I decided to give it a go and booked it. After gritting my teeth and muddling through Christmas, on January 4th 2011 I was sitting on a plane bound for Kathmandu, knowing that, at the very least, I would be contributing in a positive way to other people's lives - and forgetting about my own for a short time.

With all the events of the last six weeks still spinning around in my mind like a manic washing machine, the thought of putting myself in a situation far worse than my own seemed more appealing than lying on a beach for two weeks, living a booze soaked existence on some Mediterranean island, feeling sorry for myself.

As the plane touched down in Kathmandu, I still wasn't really sure just what I'd let myself in for; I had a million and one questions looking for answers that, deep down, I knew I didn't have. I did know I was going to be doing something positive and, more importantly, giving my time to the plight of others far less fortunate than myself. At the same time I would be scratching that itch to travel, adding another country to the growing list of those I'd visited.

After three days of sightseeing and orientation with the local volunteer co-ordinator, Asim, in Kathmandu, Nepal's colourful and bustling capital, the process of what to expect in my time at the home was explained a little more clearly. The children's home was in a remote and very poor part of the Chitwan region of Nepal, close to the border with India. I and three other 'live in' volunteers would be helping the 'House Mother,' Basanti, look after the girls and boys who lived there whose ages ranged from 5 – 14. Basanti was basically an unpaid volunteer whose husband had died some years previously. In Nepalese culture becoming a widow leads to a decrease in social standing, giving her little opportunity to find employment elsewhere. I didn't know it then, but over the next three weeks she would become my role model and a source of inspiration.

On my third day in Nepal, at 7am on a bitterly cold morning, I was put on a bus for a five hour journey, one which snaked perilously south along and over a beautiful mountain pass before eventually ending in Narayangarh, part of the city of Bharatpur. Here poverty loomed on every corner. I'd been in 3rd world countries before and knew what to expect, but even so it still takes my breath away every time I witness poverty at such close quarters. In the heat of the mid-afternoon winter's sun, people were dressed in little more than rags. Ramshackle, broken, unfinished homes made out of tin sheeting were everywhere. Children were running around, playing with whatever they could find which, though often rusty or dangerous, provided a source of entertainment far removed from anything children in the Western world would be happy with.

An hour's taxi ride from the city to the remote village of Ganganabar followed. Travelling alone and with little English spoken, I didn't have a clue where I was. On tracks barely good enough for a mountain bike, we must have hit every bump there was. Eventually, the taxi stopped outside the gates to what looked like a condemned building waiting for demolition. I hesitated, thinking there must have been some mistake, or maybe the driver was just dropping something off. But no; I had arrived at my destination.

I stepped out, put my rucksack on the floor and stared at the pink-painted house. My first thought was - 'What the fuck am I doing here?' As the taxi turned around and disappeared into the distance, I continued staring in disbelief at the dilapidated building that was to be my home for the next three weeks.

The orphanage was in a very poor area, mainly a farming community, and it seemed miles from anything even resembling civilisation. Yet all the people I'd seen on the way smiled or waved, giving the impression that they were genuinely happy to see me.

It was a shock to walk through the front door. Basanti greeted me and then gestured for me to follow her upstairs into the kitchen for a much needed cup of tea. Everywhere was utter squalor, the concrete room dusty, the windows unhinged; everything about it was totally run down. There was a concrete slab for a worktop, two gas rings, and a stone sink on the floor. The place stank of rotten food and looked as though it hadn't been cleaned in months. Surely this couldn't be classed as a kitchen? Here, apparently, it could. Behind me there was a modern looking fridge. I opened it up, mould on every seal and surface. The smell from the remains of some indistinguishable food source hit me, the opening of the door acting like bellows to waft its rotting aroma in my direction. On the stove, a pan full of water and tea leaves finished boiling and Basanti poured the hot liquid through a tea strainer into a metal cup. 'Oh, no kettle then?' I thought. After Basanti had added sugar and freshly squeezed buffalo milk, my drink was handed to me.

We then made our way downstairs to look at the rooms the volunteers would be staying in. I got one of the better ones, next to the toilet. At least this one was western style, but to flush it you had to use a bucket - and toilet paper had to go into an open bin which was then periodically emptied and its contents burned at the bottom of the garden. The walls of our rooms only went up ¾ high, so privacy would be something to forget about for a while. The shower also leaked gas every time it was turned on. This was going to be hard. As a mental picture of England came into my head, I could feel my bottom lip quivering. Then, when my own troubles reappeared in my mind, I no longer wanted to be in England. But I didn't want to be here either.

How would I manage to cope and deal with this one?

I went outside for a cigarette. Although the pink house was still standing - just - it still looked like a demolition site. Everywhere lay broken pipes and bits of bicycles; sewer water was running from a broken outlet pipe into the vegetable patch; dodgy wires poked precariously from walls and various broken gardening tools were scattered around the bare garden.

Amongst all this debris, some children were playing on a rug. I said 'hello.' I didn't know what else to say. They looked up, smiled and carried on playing with their broken toys.

Then I saw the washing machine - a stone slab with a hand pump in one corner. Children were huddled around it, squatting, washing their clothes by hand, totally focused on what they were doing, scrubbing and wringing out each item meticulously.

'You can't plug this one in then,' I thought.

I made my way back inside. Just inside the back door, I found the toilets the children and Basanti used. They were something else. When I opened the door, the smell reached out and took hold of my throat. A squat style, with no hint of recent cleaning at all, they were downright filthy and dripping water from a broken tap ran down the walls. Moving away, I looked into their bedrooms. Five, maybe six children shared a room which, quite honestly was only suitable for two. This was so depressing.

How would I cope living here? Just what had I done to myself?

I opened up my rucksack and emptied out the toys, games and books I'd brought with me from England, some my niece and nephew had given me, others I had bought myself. The children were allowed to play with them for about an hour before they were locked away in the storeroom until they were needed at some later date.

I wanted to turn and run. I was totally shocked. Here I was, a man who had spent nearly 16 years working in some of the toughest prisons in the UK - but even that had not prepared me for what I was now seeing.

I really had to get out of there, so I walked to the only bar and restaurant in the area, a lovely twenty minute walk across completely flat fields, allowing me to take the time to admire this rich lush greenery. As buffalo grazed, herons and other beautifully coloured birds fluttered above my head. It may have been winter in Nepal, but it was still warm and sunny, although it dropped to zero at night. Walking into the bar, I ordered a large beer. I needed it. I also needed to take a step back and review my situation.

After one or two more drinks, and a friendly chat with the lovely lady who ran the bar, I decided I would take a fresh look at things in the morning. To be honest, as far away as I was from civilisation, that's all I could do.

That evening two volunteers from other nearby projects arrived and after sharing several beers and a few laughs, finally I allowed myself to make the best of the situation. After all, this is what I'd wanted, wasn't it?

The next day I started to see past the squalor and see instead how they coped on a daily basis living their lives here, and how best I could help. I was surprised how they coped and dealt with everyday life in ways most in the western world would consider impossible. Over three weeks Basanti and the children taught me many qualities I didn't even know I needed to learn. They taught me patience, compassion, humanity, and how to appreciate and value what we have around us, everyday things I had previously taken for granted – like a kitchen.

There was no material greed here, only the love that the children and Basanti taught me over that short period of time. That more than made up for everything. I couldn't help but feel inspired to do something, anything, to help improve their lives. Basanti and the children had known hardship and struggle every day of their lives. Did they moan? Did they complain? No. They just got on and dealt with whatever was thrown at them.

And why? Because they had to; there was no alternative. How they did so was admirable to say the least. In fact it was amazing - and it made me sit up and think about my own situation and how best I could cope with my problems when I returned to the UK. If they could provide strength and resilience for me in dealing with everyday things, then why shouldn't I be able to overcome this blip in my life, no matter how hard it first appeared to be to deal with? All I had to do was try.

From then on, I got on with helping this one big, happy family in whatever way I could. By now there were three other volunteers around and, despite the sickness and diarrhoea bugs most of us came down with, we all worked together to do what we could. We cleaned, cooked and helped the children with their homework. I even started doing keep fit routines with the children while we were waiting for the school bus to arrive on the bitterly cold and foggy early mornings of a Nepalese winter. We painted and concreted a climbing frame into the ground - probably the most dangerous thing I'd ever seen for the use of children. We created a vegetable garden by filling in a two-metre deep hole which, apparently, was used as a swimming pool. We sweated buckets with that one, shovelling mounds of sun baked earth with little more than picks and shovels which looked like they came from a museum. It took nearly three days to fill and level a good sized plot. As the children's diet consisted mostly of vegetables, with meat as a 'treat' just once a week, this plot would be invaluable for their everyday needs.

Quite how fifteen children, Basanti and four volunteers could be fed so well was a marvel in itself. Some days were better than others, but it simply became a case of make do with what you're given – and waste nothing. So we did, although I sometimes sneaked away mid-afternoon to visit the local bar for fried rice and a couple of beers.

One day we went to the local private school that the children attended. Like so many in Nepal and India, it had very little resources and was dilapidated and run down. Even so, the children were really very happy, obviously not caring that their material possessions differed vastly from their western counterparts. They were accustomed to playing football on nothing more than a building site, filthy squat toilets that smelt even worse once the sun had warmed them up, a kitchen that was only a blackened pot and strange looking dogs scavenging for scraps in the rubbish piled high in the corner.

Whilst there I was able to observe a lesson by a Nepalese teacher. To witness the tearing up of the children's homework, the slapping of hands - or across the back - was shocking. But that is how it is here and, despite everything, the children enjoyed what little they had and nothing less than gratitude and respect was ever shown to foreign visitors, volunteers, elders and their teachers.

It was not hard to like the children here. They were all individuals with their own characteristics and traits, but there were one or two that would interact with me more than others. One of those was Tenzin, a twelve year old boy. He was so small, he only looked about eight, but he had an infectious grin and always wanting to touch or shake my hand. He often came to me for help with his homework, or to play, and he was always up at the front for our crazy early morning warm up sessions.

Bonds formed like this became more difficult to break as my time here went on. It became even harder when I was told he was to be thrown out of the home and sent back to his family a week or two later. Apparently, in the eyes of Asim and the other elders of the Brahmin caste system who were in charge of the home, he was not doing as well as he should be at school and was close to being disgraced.

Quite where this had come from, I wasn't sure but it was upsetting to hear. Kids like Tenzin deserve every chance in life. To have that taken away at this stage would surely stop him developing into a young man with opportunities.

How Tenzin and the other children coped with their lives helped me to think differently about myself. More than anything, as I settled in and accepted the surroundings, I really, really began to enjoy and embrace every new experience I was having.

Riding local buses on the roof was fun, playing volleyball over a net I made from a ball of wool was fun, kicking a football around with other volunteers and the children in the midday sun was fun, cycling around the local villages, meeting and interacting with the locals was fun. So too was helping the village elders skin and prepare a goat to celebrate a festival.

One of the funniest moments for me would be on our final night when we volunteers took all the children and Basanti to the local restaurant for a meal. Seeing these children drink Coca-Cola and then fly as high as kites was astonishing. I suppose we should have expected it, after all, with them having a mainly vegetarian diet and only water to drink, of course they would be high. Returning to the home later ensured hours of fun; fifteen hyperactive kids with eyes like saucers meant little sleep for anyone.

***

By the time I returned home at the end of January 2011 it was with a clearer head and whole load of new memories and experiences to put into my rucksack of life. It had been a memorable experience, but most of all it had been a learning curve and an adventure. As this was my first experience of volunteering abroad, I had nothing to compare it to. Settling into a way of life that was totally alien to most people was hard enough on its own, but with all the problems still banging around in my head, I knew that, when I returned home, something had to change.

Things started well enough to begin with. With my new found confidence high, I returned to work, trying to keep track on my marriage and cling to the faint hope that my wife had had second thoughts and would be returning. Not a chance, I was told.

I tried to hold things together and thought I was coping and dealing well with the pain but, by the time spring started to come into bloom, I wilted. Unable to cope or deal with the constant pressure of my career and the responsible position I held, I cracked. I could no longer bear to be at work. I was given a sick note for a month and breathed a huge sigh of relief as I now had been taken from my stressful position - if only for a short time. With this time away from work, what could I do to help myself? Well, firstly the garden got a massive overhaul. But it was during this time I first began to re-evaluate and look deeper within myself.

Who was I?

What path was I meant to be travelling down?

What was my purpose in life?

What was I meant to be doing with my life?

I'd spent the last 16 years travelling down a road I'd come to dislike more and more. Even though I held a good career, it wasn't making me happy any more. Besides which, my wife, acquaintances and nearly all things familiar were at my place of work.

I had to get away, but how?

Out of the blue, I started to work with a life coach who, by some strange coincidence, happened to cross my path around a month after returning from Nepal. Knowing I was at rock bottom, she helped by stripping me down to the bare bones of my beliefs and core values. Over the next couple of months, together we started to build me back up from there.

One noticeable question that came out of this was how I, in my own hour of need, found the strength to go to a 3rd world country and give myself to others less fortunate than me? I really didn't know. But this seemed to be another emerging characteristic I wasn't aware of. Surely it couldn't be a bad one, could it?

A new picture was evolving, emerging with every session; maybe my marriage just wasn't meant to be. I was now being sent down a completely new, unknown pathway from which I was maybe meant to find the answers I was looking for. It was around this point, by now some four months into the separation, when the idea first crossed my mind.

I had spent the last 16 years working within Her Majesty's Prison Service in England, rising to the rank of Senior Officer and, to be honest, by that point I'd had enough. There had been so many changes during my service within the public sector under successive governments - and in the prison service in particular. With the recession deepening under the coalition led government and the constant threat of privatisation looming, I was looking for any possible opportunity to plan my 'escape.' The chances of finding another job outside the civil service were slim. Because of the economic climate, people were losing their jobs and homes, so what chance would I have if I was to pack it all in and search for something new?

The solution came to me quite by chance. One day when surfing the local intranet computer system at work, a new notice to staff had come out, replacing and updating the 'Career Break Policy.' In the civil service it is possible to take a sabbatical, anything from 3 months to 5 years. Up to this point it had only been for reasons such as caring for a sick relative, but they had changed the rules and moved the goal posts. Now, anyone was eligible.

Was there was any reason why I couldn't apply?

Thinking about it further, I could take an unpaid leave of absence, rent my house out and agree a time-frame for when I'd return.

It sounded good, but how would it help me come through my situation?

Well, firstly I had absolutely nothing to lose; I could put some distance between myself and my wife, really try and heal the mind, body and soul. I could gain fresh ideas and perspectives by travelling to different countries. I could look for new opportunities; meet new people, open new doors maybe? It was a win – win situation, whichever way I turned it round and looked at it. In fact it almost seemed too good to be true. Without looking for it, this opportunity had presented itself to me. Completely sick and tired of my current situation at work and home, and being in the fortunate situation of not having any children, this seemed the best way to deal with it once and for all.

There was one problem that kept recurring though.

Me.

Even though I had gone to Nepal and returned a more penitent man than before, I was still dealing with the after effects of our separation and, even though a chink of light was starting to appear through the thick haze of mist that had clouded my mind for the past four months or so, I still wasn't sure whether I could do this.

How could I leave everything behind and head off travelling abroad?

How could I leave family and friends behind? I needed to be there for them, didn't I?

How could I take a career break? It would be too much hassle; I would miss my house, my dog, England. In fact I would miss my current life, wouldn't I?

Hang on though; didn't I want to change something?

I remembered visiting a good friend in Vietnam around two months before my wife and I split up. I can still recall the comment he made. It still resonates through me, as hard today as it was at the time. Sitting in the hot morning sun, we'd chatted over coffee. I'd mentioned that I was becoming very disillusioned with my career and that I'd fancied working abroad, doing something different with my life.

His reply still sounds powerful now. I can recall every word very clearly.

'Do you know, in all the years I've known you Phil, you're still in the same job you hate; you've talked about leaving the job and doing something different, but in all that time you have done nothing about it, you just keep repeating it every time we speak'.

Anger was my first thought. How dare he be so blunt? But when I thought about it later that morning, I realised he was right. In all the nine years or so we had been friends, I had always talked about wanting to do something else with my life, something meaningful, something purposeful - but I didn't know what. All he was doing was voicing my thoughts exactly.

I call it the 'goldfish bowl syndrome.' When you are in a situation it is much harder to take a look at what other options there are, at other ways of dealing with a problem or to look for new opportunities. Someone outside of the bowl can do that perfectly for you and, providing they are a good friend, they can do so in an objective way. That is what my friend had done – and he was right. I was doing what most people do; I talked - but took no action. If I really wanted to leave the career I was so fed up and unhappy with, only I could actually do something about it.

However, when we spoke there was one major obstacle. I didn't just have myself to consider. I was married. Little did I know that less than eight weeks later, that obstacle would be no more. With it gone, I had the opportunity to stop talking – and do something.

3
Running Against the Tide

In early April 2011, after yet another particularly unsatisfying, irritating and monotonous day at work, I returned home and finally made a decision; I would apply for the career break I had wanted. The pressures of work, combined with the on-going legal battles between myself and my wife, proved to be the hefty kick up the backside I needed. Enough was enough. Feeling like a hamster on a wheel that was forever turning but heading nowhere, it was finally time for this one to come to a halt.

I hated work. I just wasn't inspired. I didn't feel valued anymore. I longed to leave, to find or do something new. As a manager, I'd lost all faith in the 'managers' above me. In fact, they were so bad they couldn't manage a good shit in a morning, let alone manage staff. I was so disillusioned by the lack of direction the Civil Service was heading in. They would do anything to save money, being more concerned with budgets than caring about people, even to the point of endangering lives. And then there were the quite ridiculous 'political correctness' and 'diversity' hoops all staff were expected to jump through - for little more than some pointless box ticking exercise. No wonder staff began to leave in their droves, completely disillusioned by careers that had been magically transformed into mundane jobs almost overnight. In fact my own career had become 'just a job;' no wonder I was becoming desperate to change something. I felt that I had reached the end of the line where I was. After sixteen years in a high pressure environment, dealing with some really nasty people, working with the demanding and the negative, I'd had enough. After experiencing and dealing with incidents that had either upset, shocked or angered me over the years, I had now reached boiling point. There were other factors too; my wife worked in the same environment and I'd turned 40 the previous August. The combination of all these was more than enough to influence my decision.

How could I even attempt to move forward if I didn't make any changes whatsoever?

Why should I spend the rest of my working life doing something I neither enjoyed nor saw any purpose in doing anymore? I looked at that and thought of how we in the western world become caught up by what we've been told as we grow up. So many of us end up in the merry-go-round of work, home, work, not really achieving or doing anything purposeful with our lives, often ending up in drab existences with the same old routines, paying far too much tax and receiving very little satisfaction in return - only for most of us at some point to utter the immortal words - 'I wish I'd done this, or that.' A life of regret almost; I didn't fancy that.

We seem to have it instilled in us that the single most important thing to do in life is to save for years for a deposit, buy a house for an over inflated sum, and then spend the rest of our lives paying for it. So, because we spend far too much time satisfying the needs of what other people expect us to do with our lives, we don't do what we really want to do.

I remember one simple thing I was once told; 'we never actually own the home we invest so much time and money into, we only borrow it for the time we are alive on earth.' Even though I owned a house myself, I had realised some years before just how true this statement was. With that in mind I'd become conscious ever since to make sure I did as much with my life as I possibly could.

Fundamentally though, I, like most people, had hoped and

prayed that one day things would change and new doors would open for me - if I thought about them doing so for long enough. And now one had.

If you don't go through an open door, it may as well remain locked. The career break was an open door I just had to go through. It was an opportunity and I was going to take it. If I didn't, I would probably spend the rest of my life thinking - 'Why didn't I?'

The more I thought about it, the more I convinced myself it was the right thing to do. I could literally put my life on hold for a year and, if all else failed, I'd be able to walk straight back into my old job and my home.

What did I have to lose?

In a word, nothing.

***

I had a mountain of things to do, I had to make plans and take action to reduce it to a molehill. I remember how my stomach churned in knots when I made the decision to take a career break. It did even more so when I started trying to put everything into place. This was because my comfort zone was being stretched and pulled in every direction.

Scary or what?

From that moment I began to look for any new opportunity that would enhance my life in some way, however small. I stopped drinking every night. With winter turning into spring, I started running again, using Biscuit, our Jack Russell dog, as the motivation I needed, taking her for a run or a walk. I also managed to stop smoking again for the umpteenth time. Even my wife commented on how well I seemed to be dealing with our situation. Yes, damn right I was - and all because I had begun to formulate some sort of plan to deal with it. Going to work every day seemed a little easier as, at the back of my mind, I was about to give myself breathing space by doing something else for at least a year.

I then began to realise that, if I was going off to do something, it had to be different; it had to be something more than just travelling. At 40, I was probably too old to sit in backpacker bars, chilling out with gap-year students, trying to 'look cool.' I couldn't spend a year off just satisfying a wanderlust, bumming around from country to country. That wasn't for me, there had to be some real meaning attached to it. It had to be something that would not only help me, but help other people as well.

Getting involved in purposeful and meaningful work, hmm?

Trawling through the internet, looking for ideas and inspiration, I came across websites offering various programmes and projects for 'Grown-up Gap Years.' Some of their packages seemed exactly what I was after - a mixture of adventure, visiting new countries, meeting new and interesting people, doing voluntary work and of course, one of my biggest draws, working with animals. They sounded great but after looking into the cost of some of these projects, they seemed far too expensive.

"Well why not make your own up then, and just go off?" A good friend said to me when I discussed this over the phone with him. "You've already done it once. In Nepal. So, what's difficult for you?"

"That's all well and good", I replied, "But how and where do you start; it's a minefield looking on the internet."

I'd been juggling with so many things that I could feel what seemed like a simple decision turning into a headache.

"Think of a country you've always wanted to visit, but haven't yet. Find a charity or voluntary project there that you like the look of, and then look into it from there. Easy."

Well, I can't say it was easy at first. I found my comfort zone being stretched once again. I'd never travelled for longer than a month before and, to be honest, had started shitting it, thinking about the worst that could happen rather than about what would happen if I didn't take this opportunity. Despite my fears, I began to research, develop and formulate the idea that I would combine travel along with working for various charity and volunteer projects - and teaching English wherever I could too. It could potentially open new doors for the future, and that was food for thought, if nothing else.

By this time I could almost feel myself being magnetically pulled away from the Western way of living. After experiencing so much in Nepal, I was becoming so disillusioned by the disappearing core values of our society; they seemed to be so distant and very different from my own. By travelling and volunteering, I would hopefully get to know the real me. I would meet lots of new people and hopefully bring fresh ideas and perspectives into my life. Hopefully though, if nothing else, it would really open my mind to doing something different for the rest of my life.

This had to be a new beginning, a fresh challenge, a wakeup call to the soul, a way of truly finding me, who I was.

What was I really put on this earth to do?

My core beliefs would be tested, as would my inner strength and resilience to deal with whatever may stand in the way. It was a frightening thought, to head off on your own into the unknown, but it was in a good, positive way.

From that moment onwards, I regained a focus and perspective on what I was trying to achieve. Whichever way I looked at it, I knew that, if all else failed, I would return to Britain with so many new memories and experiences than I'd had before.

What an adventure! What life changing potential! Exciting stuff!

Starting to become excited by what I could achieve and the potential experiences I would have, over the next four months I planned out a rough game plan in my mind. I wanted to run with this new found momentum, so I undertook a 100 hour, Teaching English as a Foreign Language certification, giving me a new direction to follow.

What countries did I want to experience? Where did I fancy working?

As my idea progressed and started to take shape, I looked for and found a charity in Sri Lanka, a country I'd wanted to visit ever since watching the Arthur C. Clarke's 'Mysterious World series' of the 70's and 80's. I'd visited India some years before and recently been to Nepal, so I thought I may as well do the bottom bit too. The charity I found seemed a good one, small, independent, and no volunteer fee to find, but I would have to self fund and make my own way there. They were involved in a new house building project and there was also the opportunity to teach English to pre-school children. Sounding like the perfect way to start my trip, I flew to Guernsey in July 2011 to meet up with the charity's representative. I returned with a positive vibe and decided that this would become the first mapping pin, the beginning of my journey.

As the news had come through that I indeed would be granted the career break, I began the arduous task of looking at the contents of my house. What would I do with it all? I hadn't even thought about this one until now but, as a date for starting my career break was pressed for, I started hesitating, almost reluctant to commit to providing one. I again started questioning what I was about to do but, with it fast becoming a reality, I had to pull my finger out, so to speak.

So what where my options?

Well, firstly I finalised the details on the house. With a heavy heart, I'd decided that I would have to rent the house out. I didn't want to really, I'd become emotionally and physically attached to this lovely house in a beautiful area - but that was another issue. There were too many memories to not do anything about it and the longer I stayed in that house, the more upset it would make me. Renting it out would give me the much needed breathing space I needed and allow me to break the bond of the home / house syndrome. We become so attached to the materialistic image of our homes. But with my wife gone, the stark reality was this was now little more than a house. It didn't mean anything anymore. Besides, the revenue it would generate would allow me to receive a small sum every month to subsidise the savings I'd put aside for the trip.

It didn't take long to sort the details out, once I'd decided which estate agent to use. With the house taken care of and with suitable tenants lined up, I began to look at tackling the contents. I had one clear-out after another, visiting the local waste recycling plant on so many occasions, I was almost on their Christmas card list. But I had to clear the clutter and rubbish not only from my home, but also my life. So this was the start I needed. Get rid of general waste and rubbish first, I thought, then attack the personal possessions. I had decided that it wasn't worth putting furniture into storage. Firstly, it would cost too much and secondly, it wasn't worth it. Most of my things were old or had no monetary value to warrant storage fees, so there was no point squirreling it away, wasting money on looking after stuff I no longer needed. But it was too good to throw out. What could I do with it?

The following week I looked at what was left around the house.

Did I need or want it? Did I really need to keep it?

One bag followed another as I sifted through what I could pass onto others. Over several weeks, a total of eleven bags full of books, clothes, CD's, DVD's, ornaments, pictures, kitchenware and anything else that I didn't need any more, made its way to various charity shops in Harrogate. I'd supported charity shops for many years, either giving to or buying from, so it almost felt like a spiritual clear-out as I began to shed the overcoat of my former life.

Out of the blue I received a phone call from a friend at work who had also separated recently, and was looking for furniture for his new bachelor flat.

Could I help him? Yes, of course I could.

'Get round here as quick as you can, have what you want,' I said.

The timing was almost perfect. One man's trash is another man's treasure. As his van drove away from our house, I looked around the bare rooms. No sofa, TV, king-size bed, kitchenware or tables; everything we take for granted that we need – all gone.

Why would I want to hold onto material objects that now meant so little?

I could replace these at any point anyway and, after all, I certainly wouldn't need a sofa for the next 12 months, would I? I might as well let someone else benefit from my circumstances; their need was greater than mine.

By now, the date had been fixed to finish work. A week later, on the 26th September 2011, I would fly out to Colombo, Sri Lanka to begin my 'grown up gap year.' As the day of my departure loomed ever closer, the house was virtually bare. What I had kept was carefully put into boxes and stacked up, ready to be stored in the garages of my family. I had nothing left. There was no going back now.

It felt so strange at first. Everything I, or we, had worked so hard and saved to buy, memories and mementoes, trinkets or trash, all no longer needed, everything given away or discarded. But it didn't matter anymore. It actually felt good to let it all go, like a spiritual cleansing of the head, heart, and mind.

Nearly everything was in place now, yet still more things needed to be done. A week before I was due to go, I finished my last shift at work, having by now finalised my career break down to a fine art, just to keep that safety net in place for when I'd return. Walking around the place I'd given years of impeccable service to, shaking hands with people who had been acquaintances, colleagues and friends for many, many years, there was a mixture of such strong emotions, reflection, pride and sadness, yet at the same time, freedom. I could now really 'live the dream.' As I walked out of the Gate Lodge for the final time, a huge weight started to lift from my shoulders. This was it, it was real and it was happening. It was a shock, but here I was, the cocoon of job security no longer applicable.

Another moment of realisation of what I was about to embark upon was hammered home when, only five days before my last shift, a much loved and respected colleague died suddenly in his armchair at home.

"Bezzy," he had said not more than a couple of days before this happened, "If you don't do this now... I know you're worried about things not working out, but just fucking well do it. Never regret things you have done, only those you haven't. I can't wait to retire and then I'm finally out of this shit place."
Two days later, after over twenty years distinguished service to a career he'd loved, then grown to despise, he died suddenly from a massive heart attack. He had been looking forward to retirement, counting down the days – but he never got there. In that one instant I knew that life is too short. I had to take a leap of faith; I needed to forget the potential negatives and think positive. After all, it could be my turn soon. It would be someday, but when? It made me more determined to seize the moment and live in the day.

Now the day loomed ever nearer when I would have to part with probably the most precious possession from my life as it now was. My dog.

My dog, Biscuit, had been the apple of my eye for the past three years. We had adopted her when her previous owner could no longer look after her. I'd never owned a dog before, but took to looking after her like a duck to water. She had been both my and my wife's constant companion ever since. We both loved her equally but, since we'd split up, we had shared her like the custody of a child.

It had been one of the hardest decisions to make but deep down I knew that it was the only thing that still bound us together. If I was to truly move forward, then I had to sever that final tie. My wife had already said that she had wanted her permanently. It was extremely hard to deal with, but I had to accept that if I wanted to go on this trip, then I could hardly take her too, could I? If I let Gemma have the dog, then pray that upon my return maybe, just maybe, she would let me have her back? Deep down though, I knew this was a wild stab in the dark.

Five days before I was due to fly out to Sri Lanka, we stood in the hallway of our once marital home, now a bare, unfurnished shell with boxes lined up in the living room and hallway, ready to leave for the final time. We exchanged talk of what could have been, of what went wrong. Far too late for that now, I thought. Knowing how hard I'd found our separation, she commented that travelling would probably be the best way for me to deal with it and that time would be the healer I'd hoped it would be – for both of us.

I glanced down. As always, there by my feet was my loveable little dog, staring up at me, tongue hanging out of the side of her mouth, wagging her tail, hoping I was about to suggest going for a walk. Picking Biscuit up, I held her in my arms for one final time. I hugged her, told her how much I loved her and then cried and cried. The dog licked my face wondering why I was so upset. Gemma gently took her from my arms and put her on the floor. She hugged me and wished me good luck before turning around and walking out of the front door. As I watched Biscuit excitedly running after her, hoping she would be off for a walk with her mum, the tears streamed down my face. Then, with my little dog bounding about inside her car, Gemma glanced at me and waved goodbye one final time. She drove away, leaving me standing in the front porch, a blubbering, weeping wreck.

I closed the door and sobbed uncontrollably. The reality of what was coming was hitting deeper but today it had truly hit me right to the core. The stark reality of ending a chapter of your life just like that proved too difficult to comprehend at that moment in time.

The next two days were spent moving boxes and saying goodbye to friends before finally handing over the keys to the estate agents. More tears flowed as the reality that I had well and truly shut the door sank in further. Meeting my close knit group of friends over the following weekend was a sobering, yet wonderful time as we shared stories from our last 20 - 40 years together, each one wishing me luck. It almost felt like a celebration. True friends are for life and are something to treasure. Leaving my local pub, 'The Hare & Hounds' on the Sunday evening after enjoying a beer or three with the lads for the last time in twelve months, I knew that was it. Goodbye.

On September 26th 2011, I hugged my parents goodbye, the pain and grief etched deeply on their faces, knowing that their eldest son was heading off alone into the unknown to do something new, exciting and different with his life, worried that I would possibly never return in one piece - or alive even. I reassured them as best as I could, said goodbye again, then closed the door and set off with my brother to Manchester Airport Terminal 1.

Some 40 minutes later we arrived at the airport. I hugged my brother as I said goodbye. He jumped back into the car and left me and my bags at the entrance to Terminal 1. As I waved, the car disappeared from the drop zone car park, around the corner and out of view. A tear ran down my face and a lump rose in my throat. From now on, this was it, just me. My journey had begun. I was setting off to find me, maybe my purpose in life, and hopefully a new direction.

Forty eight hours later, sitting in a dreary bed and breakfast in a place called Hikkaduwa, Sri Lanka, I had finally made that big move; I had left everything comfortable, safe and familiar behind. Strangely though, as I sat there and pondered, I didn't know how I felt. I had no idea what to expect from here on in, but up to twelve months travelling seemed a big hurdle to overcome with my family and friends thousands of miles away, with no one familiar to turn to or ask for help.

Is this really what I wanted?

What would happen?

What would transpire from here - and could I cope with it?

The start of living, loving and learning about me - and the world - had begun, and now I was scared, almost terrified. This was scary stuff of course, yet it was exciting and most of all, different. I decided that I had to seize it, and I mean really seize it, make the most of this opportunity for however long it would last. I had come to realise that if you always do what you've always done, then you'll never know what you never knew. It had been time to take serious action, and I had done it, I had fucking well done it, and here I was, at the very beginning.

What would happen from here on in? Now that was a question.

4
A Stumble at the First Hurdle

The day after I'd landed in Sri Lanka, the van struggled to wind its way up the dirt track, lurching forward, then down as we hit pothole after pothole, giving my internal organs an unwanted shake-up and leaving behind us a wake of dust. I was with Sarah, the founder of the charity I was now volunteering for, making our way to visit some of the families the charity helped on a regular basis. As our van struggled to reach our intended destination, one that you wouldn't find on any tourist map, the sounds and smells from an impoverished, deprived part of Hikkaduwa greeted us. When we eventually arrived at our destination half way up a hill, I stepped out of the cool air-conditioned van into the searing Sri Lankan heat, my shirt sticking to my back almost instantaneously. The humidity here would certainly take some getting used to. Still, I might drop a kilo or two.

***

Sri Lanka had been devastated by the tsunami that hit South-East Asia on Boxing Day 2004, a disaster claiming over 280,000 lives in around fourteen countries. 2,464 of those were foreign travellers and tourists. Both Sweden and Germany lost over 500 citizens each. The third worst earthquake ever recorded, it affected the whole world in one way or another. The Tsunami's epicentre had been off the west coast of Sumatra, Indonesia where 167,799 people had died. Sri Lanka had been the second hardest hit country, followed by India and Thailand. In Sri Lanka the whole of the south-west coast had been totally decimated and 35,322 people had perished. Whole families and communities were wiped out, children were left orphaned, mothers childless and those who didn't perish were left with nothing.

The impact of losing the two biggest industries, fishing and tourism, had hit the country extremely hard. The Sri Lankan people had since had to try and pick up the pieces with very little help from their government. So help was needed fast and, since the tsunami hit, charities like Sarah's had raised significant amounts of money to do just that. It was one I had been keen to become involved with as it had really touched me. When I first looked into it, it hit home just how lucky most of us are, living in countries where we do not have to deal with natural disasters such as this tsunami.

Here in Hikkaduwa I would be delivering food and goods to families in need, helping on a new house building project and teaching English at a school in a small village close to Unawatuna, further along the coast where the charity had raised funds to build a school and create bag-making workshops to employ the local villagers, enabling them to be self sufficient.

***

The flies descended upon us as almost as soon as the van door slid open. I had been told to expect squalor, but nothing prepared me for the sight and smells that greeted me. As we walked through filth and mud, a feeling of impending doom swept across me. Sensing that this may not be pleasant, I gritted my teeth and entered the doorway of what appeared to be a pig sty. A rotting, pungent smell, what I can only describe as a mix of excrement and hot sweat, burned my nostrils. I tried to hold my breath as best as I could as I moved further into the room.

On the floor, away from the door, amongst the dirt on a flea-ridden mat, lay Granny, so malnourished she was nothing more than skin and bone, barely conscious and appearing almost dead. Even the flies had stopped coming near her. The eldest child of the family walked towards us from a room at the back, smiling happily and carrying a new born baby, the second of her two children - and she was still only sixteen years old. Then, in a room to the side, her mother, Rani called out to us. Born sightless, life had dealt her a hugely cruel blow to begin with, but to see the state of their living conditions in a house that was little more than a cattle shed and the misery this family endured on a daily basis were enough to bring a large lump to the throat. Wherever I looked, it brought the same thought - sheer deprivation. This family knew of no other way to live. It broke every humanitarian guideline ever written, yet this is the norm for thousands upon thousands of families here. Having been in Third World countries before, I had thought that nothing would shock me anymore. How wrong I was. I was speechless.

How can people live like this? How can it be right?

If the majority of the western world could see for themselves what these conditions were like; if they could see how this family live day to day - as do countless others in Sri Lanka and other Third World countries - then maybe more people would start to understand, and help more. It was so upsetting that, after we had given the family an aid parcel, I was relieved to leave. I had learnt a lesson early on; I must never again take even the simplest things in life for granted. Witnessing this first hand, even the most uncaring of souls could not have been moved by the conditions. It made me think just how lucky we are. No matter how shit your life is, it can't be any worse than that of this poor family.

***

The following day began with a five kilometre journey to the house building project I was due to start work on. Weaving through small villages and settlements as we left the comfort of the main road, the beauty of the Sri Lankan countryside opened before me like the pages of a book. I was spellbound by the sheer, vivid greenery, the vibrant colours of kingfishers darting along the river and the buffalo in the paddy fields. It reminded me so much of Nepal; it was similar in so many ways. Even the people we passed on the way smiled and waved at us - just as they had there.

I was dropped off at the building site on the edge of the jungle. I must have only been there some ten minutes before my Clima cool T- shirt clung to me with more vigour than excrement to a blanket. The humidity had introduced itself by now, and it was almost unbearable. And this was still in the low season.

Sarah introduced me to Damith her local builder.

"This is Phil; he'll be helping you over the next month" she said.

He looked at me, glanced at my hiking boots and shades, and smiled, nodding appreciatively. Typically Sri Lankan, warm, friendly, very thin and underweight, he introduced me to the gang of chirpy chappies I would be working alongside. As an ex chippie myself, this lot made me chuckle every time I laid eyes on them. They reminded me so much of the loveable rogues of the cult TV series 'Auf Weidersehen Pet' from the '80's. Damith's band of happy builders broke every 'Health and Safety' law known to man. Imagine arriving in a clearing cut from the jungle, to be greeted by seven blokes the size of whippets, leaping around, digging foundations with inadequate tools, dressed in only shorts, T shirts and broken flip flops.

'You are dressed like to go to war' one man said in broken English.

'No,' I thought, smiling at the chaps through a forehead dripping with sweat in the haze of the mid morning heat. 'I'm dressed as safely as I can be, working with you lot on a potential death trap.'

In the UK I wouldn't be allowed on any site without a hard

hat, safety boots and a high visibility vest. But here was different, this was Asia, this was Sri Lanka. Here they made up their own health and safety rules, which basically mean they don't actually exist. Yet somehow the workers know they have to be careful as there is no one to blame if they do have an accident. Nor are there the readily available doctors or hospitals we are accustomed to. So, by and large, they are careful, it's just bloody frightening to watch them hopping about. And someone falling off scaffolding is not uncommon. No wonder really, as scaffolding is little more than bamboo poles tethered together with flimsy string. It's like this throughout most of Asia; the 'building regulations' are made up as they go along, but it kind of works.

I remember chuckling to myself a couple of days later as I leant through the half finished, half square opening that would eventually house a window, watching as the shuttering for the lintels was put into place over the doors and windows. As they hammered nails into it, the whole single skin wall they'd built earlier began to shake like an earthquake was rumbling underneath.

'Hope no-one farts any time soon,' I thought, 'it would collapse.'

On the next day even more scaffolding went up as we built higher. And this scaffolding wasn't even bamboo. Trees were cut down, de-branched and tied together with rope. But it worked - somehow.

With each passing day, visible progress was being made on the building which, when completed, would be a combined house and farm shop. With it came a sense of pride and achievement.

Five days into my first project on this trip and everything seemed to be going well. The charity was purposeful and rewarding, I was enjoying the building work, and the company of the workers was fun, even if it was hard work communicating, but at least it gave me a chance to utilise some of my TEFL training. It was tiring but I knew that my contribution, no matter how small, would be making a difference to other people's lives - and that was satisfying enough in itself. At night there was usually a well earned bottle of 'Lion' waiting for me in an empty, low season bar somewhere.

But then, out of the blue, barely one week into the two month project, something happened that was to not only annoy and upset me, but also to nearly destroy my faith in what I had set out to achieve.

I have to admit it was partly my fault. A friend of mine in the UK had commented on a picture posted by the charity on a social networking site. I sent a reply through my email account and, as I assumed only my friend would read it, it did contain the kind of 'colourful' language that friends sometimes use when communicating with each other. I genuinely didn't realise that anyone in the world with internet access could read it. Naïve? Yes, I realise that now, but not at the time – and I certainly didn't mean to upset anyone.

In all the innocence that it was sent, it wasn't received in the same way by the charity. A large slice of humble pie was called for, followed by the delivery of an even larger helping of sincere apologies. Having done this, I believed that had brought an end to the matter, so I thought no more about it.

The next morning I was waiting in the oppressive heat for my lift to the jungle to appear. It didn't arrive – but a text message did, simply saying 'check your emails.' Only then did it hit me that something may be wrong. But surely not?

I returned to my hotel to check my emails and there it was in black and white. The charity had decided to remove me from all its projects, due to the comments on the social networking site. Had my face not fitted in the first place, I wondered? This made me realise that sometimes the people you have the most faith in turn out to be the ones best avoided.

The email also contained the instruction that I must return the charity's two promotional T-shirts which Sarah had given me on my arrival. I was told to drop them off at the posh, four star, all inclusive Coral Sands Hotel, where she was staying.

Well, there was a tough dilemma.

Did she really, and I mean really, expect me to drop them off after pulling a stunt like that? If she hadn't the decency to communicate with me face to face, then I'm sorry, but in my book she had lost all credibility. She must be absolutely pissed if she honestly thought I would go out of my way to drop off two $5 T-shirts. It was a choice between either putting them in the bin or using them as lavatory paper. On this occasion, and by a close call, the bin won.

I was angry, upset and now felt even more isolated. Even though I shouldn't have let it bother me, it did. But I had to face up to the fact that, as it had happened, I had to deal with it and move forward. 'I don't need her or her charity,' I thought, 'I'll just have to find one that appreciates my time and effort.' The trouble was, with my head still spinning from everything in the UK, this was the last thing I needed right now.

There's an old saying; 'shit happens'.

And it does.

When you put trips like this together, you learn vital lessons about yourself, especially when travelling alone. Everything seems magnified and becomes analysed over and over again. All the fundamentals of your faith tend to become stronger. You look at yourself in a way that you haven't done before. Certainly travelling solo can be gratifying at times, sometimes downright wonderful. Sometimes though, it can be frightening. Now, early on, and totally unexpectedly, I was finding that out the hard way.

Taking responsibility for our own thoughts, actions, movements - for everything really - gives us an underlying sense of achievement when things go according to plan and a harsh lesson in the importance of planning and preparation when they don't. Having to fight your own battles and sort out your own problems becomes something that can't be pushed to one side because, quite simply, there is no one else to do it for you; you have deal with it, like it or not. How you talk to and deal with people, how you handle each new lesson or test put in your path are all part of shaping who you are. It also pushes your boundaries, your beliefs and moves you far out of your comfort zone. This is why at times things appear frightening to us. It's not that we can't do something; it's just that we have entered the fear zone where our stomachs churn or we feel nauseous and want to run to the toilet - sometimes both. Here was a perfect example of it happening to me. Barely a week into my trip and it had all gone wrong.

So what do I do now? How do I move on from this so early into the trip?

Well, I packed my bags, left the hotel and jumped on a bus to a little place called Unawatuna, 22 kilometres further down the southern coast. I found some accommodation almost as soon as I got off the bus, only around an hour and a half after I left Hikkaduwa. I closed the door to what was to be my home for... well, however long it would take for me to gather myself together and plan my next move. I put my bags down, lay on the bed and cried. In the eight months prior to this day I had cried enough tears to fill an Olympic size swimming pool. And here I was, doing it again.

Some fifteen minutes later, I stopped.

What had I done to deserve this? What had I done that been so horrible?

Absolutely nothing, came my gut reaction.

I had learnt a cruel and harsh lesson early on. Sometimes things are not meant to work, no matter how hard we try to make them. I had to stop blaming myself and just focus on what my options would be now. I must admit I thought about saying 'sod it, I'll jump on a plane back to the UK,' but then I had to think again. I couldn't do that even if I truly wanted to. I'd taken 12 months off work, rented my house and given away virtually all my possessions. Apart from family and friends, who would have loved to see me return, I had nothing to return for.

Whichever way I looked at it, it was my choice and my decision to do something different with my life. I should have expected problems to arise. So now, just because a hurdle had been put in the pathway so early on, why should I allow it to stop me moving forward?

There was absolutely no reason whatsoever; all I had to do was formulate a plan to get over this hurdle and move forwards. I got changed and went for a walk to clear my head. All I could think of was 'what was I going to do now?' I decided that the best course of action would be to chill out for a day or two, go down to the beach, take in a tour maybe and look at my options at the same time. So that's what I did.

That night I got very drunk in a little bar on the beach called 'The Lucky Tuna.' Sinking a couple or six of the local 'Lion' lager, I met some blokes from marine security firms who, after docking at Galle, had a few days shore leave. Telling some of the chaps about why I was travelling alone and my plans, all I got were positive comments. I had to try and make this work. Stuff the charity I was meant to be working for; I didn't need any negativity right now; I had to stay positive and focus on my next move. After all, twelve months is a long time to plan out and, at this stage, I could afford to sit back and survey my options and not rush into anything. The problem was - I like to be really organised, so this would be quite tough for me.

The next day I made another decision. I had brought far too much gear to logistically carry around with me for twelve months. No way could I carry that bloody backpack everywhere, it weighed a ton. So I went to the Post Office in Galle and posted my walking boots and other surplus kit back to the UK.

Having lightened my load, I headed to the local internet café to start looking into what to do next. Firstly I visited a website called 'True Traveller' which posts links to companies or organisations looking to get people involved in purposeful travel. I'd joined them months earlier, finding some of their information quite useful. By looking through their links, I found one for 'Ecoteer,' another firm that aims to provide meaningful travel to people like myself, wishing to volunteer and gain new experiences at little, or no, cost.

I joined them and, looking for something else to get involved in, sent emails to various placement projects. I began looking at a couple of TEFL related jobs too, so I could look at teaching English. Suddenly, by taking a step back and thinking about what options may be available, there now seemed to be some light at the end of the tunnel. Feeling pleased that I had discovered some potential new voluntary opportunities in a short space of time; my self confidence began to rise again, injecting me with renewed strength and comfort.

The next day I spent at Yala National Park with two rather nice, young Russian girls. Slowly the bad experience from the previous week began to fade. It was difficult to adjust to being on my own so much; it was still low season so there weren't many tourists about. Perhaps this was why I seemed to be the only one being picked on by the locals, being asked repeatedly whether I needed a motorised rickshaw taxi, known locally as a tuk-tuk.

With tourists being the main prey of the tuk tuk drivers, they had all learnt enough English to get by. Unfortunately though, there was one word they did not understand. That word was 'No.'

"Tuk tuk?" they would ask.

"No thank you," I'd reply.

"A girl?"

"No."

"A boy?"

"NO!"

"Some weed then?"

"No"

Conversations like this happened so many times each day my patience soon began to wear quite thin. As the week progressed I had started becoming more comfortable with my own company, something you have to learn to get used to pretty damn quick when travelling alone.

By this time I had received replies from some of the emails I'd sent. Very soon I had two really interesting projects lined up. The first was at a dog and cat rescue and sterilisation centre called Lanta Animal Welfare on the island of Ko Lanta, off Krabi in Thailand. The second was teaching English to trainee Buddhist monks in Surin, North Eastern Thailand. Both had volunteer spaces available with openings from the end of October through November. I jumped at the chance and booked my places straight away. Now a plan seemed to be coming together, giving me something else to focus on.

How great that made me feel, not only in knowing I had not one, but two, new projects to look forward to, but also that I'd found the resilience and inner strength to keep motivated after my original plans for Sri Lanka had backfired so abruptly. By doing back to back projects, it meant that I would have to stay in Thailand for longer than the 30 day on arrival visa, giving me time to explore and travel the country, as well as the volunteer work.

By now, my comfort zone was so stretched, it felt like it was about to snap. I'd never been to Thailand before, so the thought of exploring its southern islands and its mainland provinces filled me with both excitement and anticipation. At least I could kick back a little now, move on from Unawatuna and explore more of Sri Lanka before flying off to Bangkok on the 20th October.

With the plan now in place, I had to take a five hour bus ride up the coast to the capital, Colombo, so that I could secure the 60 day tourist visa needed before I could enter Thailand.

After waiting for two hours for the embassy staff's lunchtime to come to an end, I completed all the relevant paperwork only to be told by the unhelpful, and less than friendly, embassy worker that I could only submit my application in a morning, so I would have to come back the next day. Bureaucratic 'jobsworths' it seems, are everywhere. My blood pressure started to rise and I could feel my frustrations threatening to boil over. But I had no choice. I would have to stay in Colombo and come back the next morning. So I needed to find somewhere to stay for the night. Being Colombo it wasn't cheap, and with me being a Lancastrian, that's all I wanted, somewhere cheap and cheerful.

I did find cheap – but it certainly wasn't cheerful. Sitting in the filthiest, yet cheapest, option in town, the YMCA on Bristol Street, Colombo, I learnt another lesson:-

Don't be a tight bastard, look at where it can get you.

After an awful night's sleep in the YMCA, being woken by the buzz of mosquitoes or the unrepentant sound of constant traffic outside my window, not to mention the stench from the bathroom or the smell of the pillow, it crossed my mind that, had the Village People stayed here, they wouldn't have been so enthusiastic to write a song about it.

Leaving the YMCA behind, I duly reported back to the visa office and submitted my passport. Having then been told to return three days later, I bound a bus heading for Kandy.

Kandy is a bustling and vibrant city, steeped in ancient history and slap bang, right in the middle of the country, perfect for using as a base for exploring both the Hill Country and the Cultural Triangle. Learning from my YMCA experience, I upgraded myself and stayed in a lovely guest house, giving me a couple of days to look at what Sri Lanka had to offer.

Over the next couple of days I took in the Temple of the Tooth, which holds the Relic of the tooth of the Buddha, Pinnawala Elephant Orphanage, Udawatta Kele Wildlife Sanctuary and the Peradeniya Botanical Gardens. I also climbed the quite breathtaking Sigiriya Rock and visited the Dambulla cave temples.

On the third day I returned to Colombo to collect my visa and, after nearly eight hours and 220 km of travelling, returned to Kandy, looking forward to tomorrow. I had planned to head off and try something which I hoped would help clear my head and dispel some of the built up anger and stress from the past year. I was going to study meditation.

***

There is something very endearing about travelling on local transport in Asia. Apart from being ridiculously cheap, it is a great way to see the country, in the way the locals do. To be honest it's amazing to watch how people are crammed onto these buses in a way that you just wouldn't think possible. Just when you think it's full, the conductor, carrying his book of tickets, will jump off the bus at the front, run round to the back, shout something in Singhalese and then proceed to pack on at least half the amount of people who were already hanging onto every pocket of air available, into what space he seemed to have found.

As the bus weaved its way towards Nillambe Junction, where I was going to study meditation for the next two days, I was perilously thrown from my seat at every corner, finding myself crushing a poor granny into the window one minute only to find a gentleman's crotch forced into my face the next. Travelling at 40 miles an hour, I watched in disbelief as, on more than one occasion, the driver would overtake another bus on a blind bend.

"No thanks," I gestured at the tuk tuk drivers as I stepped off the bus an hour later, stretching my sore legs. "I'll walk."

I'd been so cramped up for much of the journey; a walk seemed a good idea. Forty minutes later, as I wrung out my T-shirt again and with still no sign of my destination way up in the hills, it didn't seem such a good idea any more. I now realised why the chaps in the tuk tuks were laughing at me when I had declined their offer to take me up to the Nillambe Meditation Centre.

Eventually though a sign appeared saying 1000 metres. Wrong. It wasn't long before I wondered whether the sign-writer had run out of paint or just knocked off early. Either way there must have been a nought missing.

Climbing further, the views were stunning and, when I eventually turned up dripping wet at the Centre's green gates, I'd convinced myself it had been well worth the walk after all.

The monk in charge greeted me warmly, welcoming me to the centre and giving me a pillow, a pillow case, two blankets and four candles as he checked me into my home for the next two days. I did see a couple of other people walking about, so at least I knew I wasn't going to be here alone.

"Please, follow me" he said.

He led me down some stone steps, past the washroom and into a bare building which housed the male meditators.

"This is your room," he said.

I opened the door into a 10 foot x 5 foot room, a 'Kuti' as they are called in Buddhist circles - or a prison cell as they are called in mine. 'Nice and compact,' I thought. 'Minimalist is the term, I think.' But it was a vast improvement on Colombo's YMCA, so it was enough for my needs for a couple of nights. Each Kuti contained a bed, a corner table, a shelf, three coat hooks, a window and an assortment of insects and creepy crawlies. Oh well, I'd just have to get used to my room-mates - just as I would have to get used to 'Noble Silence.'

Being a typical westerner, I didn't realise the centre operated the policy of 'Noble Silence.' After spotting the first person I saw, I proceeded to shout across the courtyard, 'How's you?' When all I received by way of a reply was a cursory smile and a finger pointing to the sign that itself pointed this little oversight out, I realised that lots of self discipline would be needed to get me through the hardship of a self-imposed silence.

Never mind, at least talking to myself wouldn't appear so daft after all - and at least I would win every argument.

The concept behind Noble Silence is that, by being alone with your thoughts you can connect with yourself and the universe on a higher level and, by connecting to this silence, the person can become more 'noble' through being bright, positive and feeling everything around them at this heightened level.

To my surprise, I found the experience of living a simplistic existence to be invaluable; I learnt so much about self-discipline. Living high up a mountain side, being eaten alive by leeches and eating only vegetarian food three times a day, with no alcohol or cigarettes, was not as bad as it sounded - so much so that, after the first day of meditating and not talking, I went to bed at 8 o'clock and I slept like a log for the first time in a very long time - and what vivid dreams I had too.

As 5 am broke on the Monday morning and the first of the day's call to prayer and meditation began, I actually thought about extending my stay for another day. But, with my flight booked to Thailand only three days later, I still had other things I needed to see and do before then. Bidding a fond farewell to the centre, I got a lift back to Kandy and then took a bus up to Nuwara Eliya, high in the Hill Country.

The day before I was due to leave for Thailand, as I walked across one of the many tea plantations near the highest town in Sri Lanka, I glanced around at the impressive landscape and started to contemplate just what I had learnt from my experiences over the past three and a half weeks.

What had I learnt? What had I thought about the journey so far?

I'd begun to realise that my inner strength had been needed far earlier than I'd expected it would be and that I had needed to pull every ounce of resilience, self-motivation and belief out of myself. I also had to have faith in my ability to cope with the initial setback and disappointment of my first volunteering experience and to deal with the reality that I was truly on my own, so that every move, decision and plan would be of my own doing. Standing here gazing at tea plantation after tea plantation, breathing in the fresh mountain air, I realised I had taken a lot of responsibility for my own actions. And do you know what? I felt rather proud of myself.

The next night as I sat in the departure lounge of Sri Lanka's airport awaiting my flight early the following morning, I wondered what fresh challenges awaited me. I looked ahead to the next two months in Thailand. With two charity projects to occupy my time, in a country I was eager to visit, I just couldn't wait to board that plane.

5
Mad Dog and an Englishman

Four and a half hours into the flight from Sri Lanka, as the plane began its descent into Bangkok Airport, I gazed out of the window to see the devastation of the mass floods which had started without warning three weeks earlier. Field after field, road after road lay ruined and decimated by the worst flooding to hit Thailand for fifty years, leaving over four hundred people dead in its wake. It made me think just how lucky we are in England to rarely experience rain as ferocious as this. When extreme weather hits, the impact it has on those involved, and the after effects when the clearing up begins, stays for a long time. And it wasn't over yet; it still hadn't stopped raining. Panic was beginning to set in as the airport and Bangkok city itself were potentially at risk of flooding.

After touching down I spent a rather frustrating hour and a half queuing to get through a very efficient, but painfully slow, immigration control. I had an hour long fight still ahead of me, to Krabi on Thailand's south west coast. By the time my three month entry visa was finally stamped, it left me with little more than an hour to rush around looking for Air Asia's check in desk.

The baggage collection point at Krabi airport allowed me to touch base with fellow travellers. Sharing a taxi into the town to catch the ferry shuttle bus, we swapped stories of sleeping on airport floors or on buses that smelled of wee. It seems this is quite common in Asia, although I hadn't had the pleasure of that one before. Once dropped off at the ferry terminal, I took the twenty minute journey to the island of Ko Lanta, eventually ending up at Lanta Animal Welfare Sanctuary on Prae Ae beach. By the time I arrived it was the middle of the evening; I was tired and in serious need of an alcoholic uplift. I was also in need of a quick spray of deodorant as it had been well over twenty-four hours since I'd last showered and I was worried that even flies wouldn't come near me.

After receiving a warm greeting from the manager, Jon, I was put on the back of a moped and taken to join the other volunteers currently helping out at the centre. They were, in true traveller tradition, enjoying an opening night party with beer and free food at a local bar. Warm, friendly introductions and greetings followed. What a great bunch they were, a real mixed bag of ages and experiences, all with tales to tell about how great this animal sanctuary really was. It was good for me to meet people with the same passion and desire to help animals - and people too. This, I thought, could be a really good experience; I was really looking forward to my month of volunteering here. I would be getting free accommodation in return for a six hour shift, six days a week, either 7am till 1pm or 1pm till 7pm. That sounded great as it would still leave plenty of time for exploring the 30km long and 6km wide island - its beaches, markets, diving and, of course, its night-life.

I could tell straight away that Ko Lanta was a hidden gem. It was nearing the start of high season and it was still quiet. Although it does get busy in the high season, it still manages to breathe, which means that getting around the island is surprisingly easy and pleasurable, nothing like the heaving, sweaty, hustle and bustle of the mainland - or many of the Thai islands around the Andaman coastline or Gulf of Thailand. Even better I thought, it would help to make the volunteer experience so much richer, knowing it would feel more personal. Not being pestered by tuk tuk or taxi drivers made it even more pleasing, a welcome change after the continual onslaught on myself and every other western meal ticket in Sri Lanka. When walking around, I wanted to relax and enjoy this new experience without being hassled at every turn.

The next morning I was given a tour and induction into how the centre operates, the daily routines, and various jobs involved in looking after the twenty-five cats, twenty-five dogs and five puppies in their care. Lanta Animal Welfare Centre, or LAW, was set up by Junie, a Norwegian lady who also owns the 'Time for Lime' restaurant on the island. She had originally run LAW from the back of the restaurant but it had since outgrown itself; so two years ago she opened this purpose built facility. The centre's main priority is population control. This is vital on an island the size of Lanta. The humane sterilisation undertaken here, and in similar centres, helps to reduce breeding. There is a huge problem with stray cats and dogs throughout Asia and it is common to see many strange configurations of breeds within one dog. Dogs sometimes breed within their own gene pool too. This is not only dangerous; it actually shortens the offspring's lifespan.

The centre also provides education for local people on how to look after animals and take responsibility for them. Veterinary graduates from the UK and around the world can also gain invaluable experience here before looking for work, improving their CV's in a positive way. With the centre housing around twenty-five unwanted, stray dogs including the odd three-legged wonder like Tarzan, means there are always cute, playful and adorable dogs needing a new loving home. Several of the local ex-pats have given a home to a dog or cat, as have some of the large Swedish population living and working on the island.

As costs are considerable, without donations from tourists, travellers or benefactors, the centre could simply not afford to run. For that matter, the volunteers who give their time at LAW amazed me. There was never a shortage of animal loving travellers wanting to come here and help, so I considered myself lucky to have found this opportunity as there were so few spaces when I initially applied.

Without willing volunteers many thousands of charities around the world would grind to a halt overnight. How proud every volunteer should feel, wherever in the world and in whatever capacity they freely give their time. Volunteering becomes so enriching in so many ways and provides life changing experiences, ones that I, for one, will ever forget. Now I had become a volunteer here, I was really looking forward to getting stuck in and helping in any way I could.

With the humidity and heat, the work took some getting used to but it was enjoyable and the environment so pleasant to work in. Even dealing with dog shit in 30 degree heat was bearable. All the other volunteers were really good people, all with the sole purpose of improving the animals' lives. I settled in really well. This was the much needed breath of fresh air I needed after the sour taste of Sri Lanka; so much so that, when Jon asked me to walk Sanchez two days after my arrival, I jumped at the chance.

Sanchez was a pretty nondescript dog, what you might call a 'Heinz 57 variety' - a mix of all sorts. He came to Lanta Animal Welfare Sanctuary after he'd been found roaming the streets. He had a chunk of fur missing from his collar area where he'd been involved in numerous street fights with other dogs and come off second best. Classed as a high risk dog, he was not allowed to run in a pack like most of the other residents. Instead he was kept in a kennel on his own and needed to be walked with care, using a strong lead and harness.

"Just be careful," Jon said. "He's a bit unpredictable; he's slipped his harness before, hates other dogs and cats and if he sees them, he'll start whimpering. If he does, just turn around and bring him back."

No problem, I thought, I'll just talk to him if anything happens and he'll be okay.

That was my first mistake.

Dogs like this old boy don't listen, they just react on impulse. And guess what? Only a mere five minutes into our lovely stroll and on only my second day as a Lanta Animal Welfare Volunteer, he took me on a walk I wouldn't forget in a hurry.

We set off along the track from the centre towards the main

road that circles the island. As I thought about how good it felt to be relaxing, taking this dog for a bit of a stroll, I heard a 'yap, yap' come from a nondescript ball of fluff some hundred yards in front of us. 'Oh, there's a little dog down there,' I thought. I think it was a Lhasa Apso or similar, a tiny little thing and no obvious threat to this big daft lump.

That was my second mistake.

Never underestimate the thought processes of a dog, especially one you don't know. Without warning, Sanchez let out the most ungodly whimper and howl I've ever heard, quickly pulling down hard on his lead and nearly pulling it from my grasp. I thought this must be what I'd been warned about. Jon's words, 'just turn around and bring him back,' echoed in my mind. But before I could tell Sanchez that was the plan, he again leapt up and howled like a banshee, slammed back down onto his paws and, after doing a little shimmy, like a canine Houdini he had slipped his harness and was free. I couldn't believe what I'd just witnessed.

'Sanchez, come here!' I shouted.

It was no use; this daft old dog was not as daft as I thought. He had just seen a new toy to play with, although, for some reason, I knew that play was the last thing on his mind. Having escaped from his harness, he was off, running as fast as he could and the little doggy in the distance had now become a moving target. He chased him some hundred yards towards the little dog's home, a bamboo shack. He caught him under the shack, gripping him ferociously in his powerful jaws, shaking the poor creature like a rag doll. I caught up slowly as my sandal strap had broken while running after him. I shouted and waved at him but it was having no effect whatsoever. He was totally fixated on his quarry and, now he had caught what he wanted, no amount of reasoning was ever going to stop him.

Deep down I knew there was only one way Sanchez would ever stop but I didn't want to imagine that. Not now, please. Grabbing a length of bamboo from the floor, I tried from every angle possible to get to him under the bamboo table he had slid underneath. A horrible curdling whimper came from the little dog; I could see that by now his neck was exposed and his life was ebbing away at a rapid rate, but still Sanchez would not let up on his poor victim, shaking and biting down even harder on the dog's throat.

I tried various non-verbal communications with the little dog's owner and he also tried unsuccessfully to help grab the big dog. Then, as suddenly as it had all started, Sanchez backed away leaving a lifeless ball of fur lying in the dirt underneath his home. By this time Jon, the manager, had arrived. He scooped the injured dog up and rushed him back to the centre's surgery. Despite the frantic efforts of the centre's vets, the poor dog died soon after.

I was absolutely devastated. Just two days into my new project and I had let a dog slip its harness and destroy another one. After the earlier issues in Sri Lanka, I wondered whether this trip would also be blighted the whole way through. Even though Jon reassured me that Sanchez was totally unpredictable and that it could have happened to anyone, I still blamed myself for him slipping his harness and killing a dog. I turned it over and over in my mind on that Saturday evening.

What could I have done differently?

What could I have done to prevent it happening?

The same answer kept on returning. Nothing. I had to accept that it happened, that it could have happened to anyone, and move on. Again another harsh lesson learnt - you can't teach an old dog new tricks and, shit, didn't I know it? I still felt bad but I had to pick myself up and carry on. I'd come here to help these animals the best I could. Now I needed to get over this wobble and concentrate on helping and giving my best to the sanctuary.

***

A couple of days later, I was playing pool in a bar. I ended up playing a chap named Ross, an Irishman from Dublin who was travelling around Asia and visiting most of the countries I'd also planned to visit. As we shared three or four beers, we chatted about our travel plans, amongst other things.

"If you're looking at doing something completely different, why don't you try walking the Camino de Santiago, or the Way of St. James as it's also known?" he asked as we mentioned personal challenges and overcoming parts of our lives that had caused pain and upset.

After confessing that I'd never heard of it and didn't have a clue what it was, he started to explain to me how he had done this old Catholic pilgrimage not once, but twice in the last eight years and that it was one of the best things he had ever done.

"Allow 35 days to do it," he said. "You fly to Biarritz in France, then catch a train down to the start. It goes all the way from Saint Jean Pied de Port, across the Pyrenees and then the whole of Spain, ending up in Santiago de Compostela. It's around 800 kilometres long, but I tell you, you won't regret it, Phil. I met some of the best people I've ever met in my life and I've become great friends with them. This will change your life in so many ways and it sounds like it's just what you'd enjoy too."

Suddenly the idea became more than just an idea. It was something I could do after this trip was over, something big, something again to aim for. It would need some planning but it was certainly achievable. Maybe it could be the spiritual clear-out I needed?

"Plenty of people do it for that reason, Phil. They all have such great stories to tell of personal grief, loss, overcoming illness or trauma - or just a new challenge for their own benefit. You should definitely give it a go."

The more the conversation - and the beer - flowed, the clearer the image and idea became. After all, what was I doing with this trip now? I was pushing myself, pushing my boundaries, pushing my limiting beliefs about myself and what I could potentially achieve with my life. I had made all this possible by wanting change, by becoming aware of choices and challenges, by looking for opportunities to enhance myself in any way. Surely

I'd done the hardest part by opening my mind and taking strong actions to make this trip a reality. So I knew I could achieve it.

Without even looking for it, another new challenge had opened its doors to me. Without even questioning myself further, I just knew I had to do the pilgrimage. I knew I wanted to. This time I could almost see the opportunity to enhance my life even more and, as a result, potentially influence people I hadn't yet met in a way I could never have imagined. With all the talk of the Camino, the pool games just dragged on and on. This could be good, I thought, but no need to worry about that yet, leave it in the memory bank for later. I left the bar that night with an upbeat and vibrant feeling, Oh by the way, the pool game ended in a five-all draw.

***

Another new experience I'd forced myself to take since arriving on Lanta was the hiring of a moped. Even though I'd never ridden anything with a motor before, much preferring a chain and handlebars to an engine, I'd resigned myself to the fact that the only realistic way to see this island and get around independently would be to bite the bullet and hire one.

The day after the motivational game of pool with Ross, I was sitting astride my Yamaha Mio twist and go scooter. Wobbling along the winding Kantiang Beach road at dusk, I really did feel like Peter Fonda in 'Easy Rider.' With my shades and rather 'cool' lime green helmet, here I was burning up the miles, feeling as free as a bird, soaking up and enjoying every new minute of riding this little bike.

I began to think back to some of the Ewan McGregor and Charley Boorman 'Long Way' books I'd read which had really helped to influence my decision to travel for twelve months. I thought of how they must have felt riding through the different countries and over the various challenging terrains they had encountered on their journeys. I almost felt like part of the books or the TV series as I saw the island in a new and exciting way. As I wound up the throttle to a full 40kmph and thought back to the previous night and all the events of the trip so far, I decided there and then I would not return to my previous life. Not only had I begun to make changes to my life, I had also realised what possibilities and opportunities had already started to open up. I had to keep going, no matter how hard it might be along the way.

This was a journey; wasn't that what I wanted? For the first time in the trip, I now felt relaxed and at ease. I was enjoying this new experience of riding a moped and, for a short time, convinced myself that I actually did look pretty damn good on that scooter, especially with that helmet.

***

Three weeks into the voluntary project and it had been a heady mix of work, beer and more beer. So, on my day off in the week, I headed off to do something different, away from the smells of dogs and cleaning products, something I enjoy doing when travelling. Diving. A keen diver, I'd done my PADI Open and Adventure Diving courses in Australia some years previously. Since then I'd seized any opportunity to collect fun dives from my travels.

As the dive boat headed out from the harbour at Saladan towards Koh Bida, the wind whistled around my balding pate. During the trip I discovered that the dive master in charge of the boat actually drank in the same pub as I used to back in sunny Lancashire. I managed a sly chuckle to myself about how strange that was. As a German girl had said to me one night in Sri Lanka; 'The world is a village'. How little did I know just how true that phrase actually was.

These past three weeks had been some of the most enlightening of my life so far. My contribution in helping out here was worth more to me than money could buy. I had met some lovely people from all corners of the globe; I had formed a great bond with the animals and become involved in a charity project which was not only stimulating but incredibly fulfilling, knowing how we were making a difference to the animals' lives. Even the day before the diving, I'd gone into the kitchen to start work and found a gecko stuck to fly paper on the bench. It had obviously been there for some time. Seeing animals in distress is not my thing and, after finding out that cooking oil works well on fly paper, I proceeded to gently hold the little fella and rub his little paws with oil until one by one, he became free. What a feeling to have saved his life. If he had stayed there much longer he would have died - or one of the cats would have eaten him. Putting him down on the worktop, he set off on his travels once again, free to live his life, doing what a gecko does.

As we sped across the Andaman Sea I actually felt a lump in my throat as I thought about a very special friendship I'd made here. The day I arrived in the centre, I met a frightened, timid puppy named Becks. He virtually lived in our kitchen and he was so petrified of human contact that any noise would see him shaking with fear.

"Why is he like that?" I asked.

I was told that, since he had been found, he had been unable to interact in any way with any of the volunteers. It was so obvious he'd been abused as he wouldn't allow anyone near him. So there was virtually no chance of him ever being fostered or adopted.

I saw that as the ultimate challenge; the gauntlet had been thrown down. But, what could I do to help him? I wasn't really sure - but I decided that, from that moment forward, I would make it my mission to help him as best I could. I just knew I had to help this poor little frightened soul to become a dog and enjoy his doggy life. My mission had begun. Hopefully in the process it would help heal my sense of loss after having to give up my own dog.

Caring for the majority of the animals here was just a matter of providing their basic needs. But a small minority also needed some extra TLC. I decided that, in Becks' case, I was the man to give it. Every spare moment I had I threw into gently trying to coax and interact with him, but to no avail. He wouldn't respond to anything. What made it more frustrating was that I could see the love in his little brown eyes wanting to come out and the actual 'want' to behave like a dog, to go on walks, to be cuddled and fussed over, to be stroked and loved. But such was the severity of the physical and mental torment he had suffered in the four months of his short life, he was afraid of any form of human contact. I began to think it was a fruitless challenge.

Slowly but surely though, I began to get through to him. Every day after I'd finished my shift, I'd go into his kennel, sit on the floor and let him smell my hand. After the first week we managed to catch him and put a collar on him - something that resulted in Becks defecating and trying to bite us.

Defecation was repeated quite regularly, every time he was approached or handled. The collar helped control him, yet he still needed so much work. He must have been one traumatised dog. We needed to get him out of the kitchen and into an animal surrounding, so he was housed in the puppy enclosure at the back of the kennels. Little by little, eventually Becks would allow me to pick him up, put a lead on him and then put him down on the ground - but he still wouldn't walk on a lead.

Then, in the third of my four weeks at LAW, came a breakthrough. It came in the form of another dog, Stella - Becks' sister. She had been fostered but, for some reason, had now ended up back with us. One day, another volunteer had hold of Stella - and I had Becks.

"Just start walking" I said.

When she did, slowly Becks lifted his little head up and, curious as to what Stella was up to, he started following her, taking his first few faltering steps on a lead. This was it - the breakthrough I had been searching for so frustratingly over the past few weeks.

From that moment on, and for the remainder of my stay there, Becks got better and better every day, so the hard work and patience finally paid dividends.

***

It seemed that, no sooner than I'd arrived here, it became time to leave. The last four weeks had indeed been a heady blur of hard work, new friendships made, a shared mission to help animals and of course, consuming enough alcohol to drain a brewery. The experience had definitely been more than worthwhile, giving me another amazing experience to carry in my ever-growing rucksack of life.

Before leaving I went around the kennels one last time, saying goodbye to Dok-Dek, Tarzan, Michael, Punk, Owen, Lucy, Rufus and all the dogs who had become attached to their 'Uncle Phil.' One by one I hugged them all, fussing over them for the final time. It became one of the hardest moments in my life to pull away from one of the few things in life that gives such unconditional love. Only a mother's love comes close to the love an animal gives you, freely given without wanting anything in return.

I went into the puppy enclosure to say goodbye to my little protégé. I bent over and Becks licked my hand, as he'd done so many times over the last four weeks. I picked him up; he lay in my arms, gazing up at me, motionless but happy. I cried. I cried over the bond I'd formed with him and I cried because of the loss of my own dog; I cried as, at 41 years old, I was now becoming more in touch with my emotions and feelings than I thought I'd ever be; I cried because once again I was moving off again into the unknown, leaving the comfort and safety net of a place that every day generated so much love and positivity.

"Keep in touch Phil. Good Luck and thanks for everything you've done with Becks; it's amazing!"

Amongst all the hugs and kisses, these words whizzed around my head as the Air Con bus passenger door opened and I reluctantly climbed on board. As the bus pulled away and made the slow journey towards the ferry port, I afforded a wry smile to myself as I remembered the pack of six dogs that had ripped my beloved Bury FC football shirt to pieces – when it fell as it was drying above their pen. Shaking my head slowly, I thought; 'They must support Manchester United, little buggers.'

Next stop Surin.

6

Whoa, Whoa, Whoa, Sweet Child O' Mine

As my flight touched down in Bangkok, I wondered just what I'd let myself in for on the next leg of my adventure. Teaching English to novice monks had caught my attention as it was an ideal opportunity to put my TEFL certification to the test. It would certainly be a challenge as it was something I had never done before.

I settled onto the air-conditioned Nakonchai Air bus for the journey that would take me to the North Eastern Thai province of Surin. After the recent flooding, I had expected a long and arduous trip but, seven uneventful hours later, I arrived at Surin's bus station virtually unscathed. There I was met by June, a lovely Thai lady who was the volunteer co-ordinator and co-founder of Lemongrass Volunteering, the company in charge of supplying volunteers to Thai schools desperately in need of native English speakers. Even though I was tired after my day's travel, I was eager to get stuck into teaching English to monks.

As I was being driven through the streets in a tuk-tuk heading towards the volunteers' house, I could see that Surin was a thriving, bustling place, one typifying the sheer beauty and delights that South East Asian towns and cities have to offer. Insects swarmed in their thousands in the luminous glow of the street lamps lighting up the night markets crammed full of food stalls. By the roadside, people were happily chatting to friends, laughing and joking or playing cards and swigging whisky. A heady aroma hung in the air, a mixture of that coming from the food stalls and that from the rubbish piled high on the roads.

Arriving at the volunteers' house, I was introduced to Emma, a volunteer who came from Eastbourne in England. I was told that, over the next couple of weeks, the two of us would be the only volunteers. Emma had already been here for a week and, over a cup of coffee and a cigarette, she told me about her experiences so far, of how she was enjoying the challenges of teaching English as a second language to the 6 – 12 year olds (grades 1-6) at two local state run schools, Baan Gaeyai and Baan Dhaban.

The following day I was introduced to June's partner, Adrian, a likeable chap who, like me, had been on a journey of self-discovery some five years earlier, meeting June whilst on his travels. They'd become a couple and three years later they set up Lemongrass Volunteering. Apologetically he told me that there had been a technical hitch and I would not now be teaching English to trainee monks, I would instead be teaching at the same two schools as Emma.

Okay, not quite what I'd expected but, nevertheless, still a great opportunity to put into practice my hard earned 100 hour TEFL certificate. Other than in-house training programmes and first aid courses at work, I had never taught before so any experience would be more than beneficial, especially if I were to make a career of it in the future. Making a living working abroad certainly has its attractions. If I could do a good job and take to teaching maybe I could look at becoming a full time TEFL teacher at some point? Another thing to think about maybe?

Before sitting down to think about and prepare a lesson plan for three classes the following day, my first at Baan Gaeyai school, I rode rather gingerly around Surin, checking out all the amenities on my new, rather fetching mode of transport. For the duration of my stay I had been given a lovely, single gear beauty of a 1970's bicycle, complete with shopping basket and a

'Famous Five' style bell. With every pedal turn, I prayed it wouldn't disintegrate.

That evening, I discussed with Emma my thoughts, fears and expectations about teaching English. I'd prepared what I'd thought would be a great lesson plan but, as I had no idea of what level the students were at, there was nothing for it really, I just had to get in there, give it a go and see what happened.

***

Clutching my bag with my prepared lessons and materials, I walked through the gates of Baan Gaeyai School for the first time, ready to be let loose on a classroom full of children between the ages of 9 and 12. At 8.30 in the morning, crowds of smiling happy faces ran to greet us as the tuk-tuk dropped us off inside the school gates. It was evident most of these children came from poor backgrounds, their clothes were either unwashed or torn and some even had no shoes on their feet. Even so, I couldn't help but notice just how happy they were.

Looking around the school and glancing into the classrooms, I realised that, compared to western schools, those here were basic and unfinished. Even so, they were places of learning, and the local teachers did the best that they could with the resources they did have. As the local authorities couldn't afford to employ native English speakers, volunteers from Lemongrass, or other volunteer organisations, were used instead, giving the children the opportunity to learn valuable English skills before they went to secondary school at 12 years old.

The night before I had spent two hours meticulously preparing and sweating over a lesson plan for three one-hour lessons in grades 4, 5 and 6. I had prepared the same plan for all the age groups, tailoring the activities to suit the children's ages and abilities. Armed with this, I was thrust in, as they say, at the deep end, to teach my first class of children. Would I sink or swim? Could I now actually cut the mustard as an English

Teacher? Well, I was about to find out.

**

After two of the three lessons, I met up with Emma at lunch. She wanted to know how my first morning had gone.

To be honest, I'd struggled. It had been much harder than I thought it would be. As their level was not as high as I'd expected, my lesson plan was too advanced - and there were well over thirty pupils in each class. Even so, it had gone as well as I could have expected it to. Everything I had learnt on the TEFL course was put to the test. I knew my lessons had to be informative, educational and, above all, fun. So, trying to keep the focus of my young and easily bored learners, I'd leapt around the classroom like a demented madman on speed.

After those first two lessons I'd realised just how hard the next three weeks were going to be. Could I rise to the challenge? 'Yes,' I thought, 'damn right I could. But I was certainly going to have my work cut out.' That night, over a welcome beer or three, I looked to devise a suitable battle plan to help me through it. Overall, day one had gone reasonably well, I just needed to overcome my lack of teaching experience by preparing accordingly and adjusting to each class. I had to let it flow and try my best. After all, what was the worst that could happen?

**

Surin is a typical Thai city and home to the famous 'Elephant Festival' every November. It has a population of around 41,000, yet it's small enough to feel like a town and it has everything the average 'Farang' - the rather quaint colloquial term locals give to foreigners - could possibly need. Over the next couple of weeks Emma and I explored the markets, egging each other on to try the various local delicacies – a kind of self imposed 'bush-tucker trial.' Ant and Dec would have been proud of us as we

69

chewed on, and forced down, deep fried locusts, grasshoppers, crickets, red ants and anything else we spotted which we fancied giving a go. Spending the evening sampling the local beer and street food at minimal cost, combined with the enjoyment of teaching to enthusiastic yet impish classes of between 22 and 37 children during the day, really gave me a sense of how enjoyable this working lifestyle in Asia could be if I decided to make it a reality on a regular basis.

Another great thing about Surin was the distinct lack of other 'Farangs,' as it isn't on a regular backpacker route. After the month spent on Ko Lanta, where tourists were everywhere, it was strange at first to adapt to living in a city off the tourist map but I soon found that it made the experience so much richer - in every sense of the word. I could observe better how the local people went about their daily lives. It was fun to communicate and fit in with the local community. The few Thai words that Emma and I had learnt were warmly received by just about every person we spoke to. The novelty factor of us feeling like a spot on a domino was really evident but rather endearing at the same time. We were often pointed at and the subject of stares but, like the experience of eating fried locust, it was something we just got used to. Only by making the effort and trying to fit in to the Thai way of living was I able to experience up close and personal how the milk of human kindness flows freely throughout the world. If we allow ourselves to let it, how easy it is to drink from the same cup as the locals.

***

There were some truly frustrating moments in class when the kids didn't understand my thick Lancastrian accent. I'd begun to tear out what little hair I had left until I realised that I would have to speak slowly, clearly and above all, in a neutral accent. Then the children understood better and, as a result, learnt more. With that, the experience of teaching English as a second language became more pleasurable and rewarding. As my confidence grew, the lessons gradually began to flow more freely and the more fun they became. It gave me the opportunity to really connect with the children. Even better, it gave me the chance to act like a complete prat for three hours a day, making silly noises, getting the kids on their feet exercising at the start and end of every lesson, pretending to be characters off 'Little Britain,' 'The League of Gentlemen,' 'Phoenix Nights' and whatever else I could think of to illustrate my points. And guess what? The kids loved it. Seeing 'Teacher Phil' running around the class, during a lesson on 'feelings' as I demonstrated 'hot, tired, excited and scared' would be enough for any small child to suffer from nightmares - and report back to their parents that their new English teacher was a complete nut job. Quite often, during my mad hour's teaching, I'd throw in a couple of song titles or the chorus from a random rock classic, as a way of engaging the class. This had the added bonus of giving me the opportunity to sing. Now, singing has given me a large amount of pleasure over the years. Unfortunately it is something I am notoriously dreadful at; so much so that, in the past, it had led to a self imposed ban on karaoke. As my friends had regularly pointed out, this was a real blessing.

Overall the teaching, and everything else for that matter, was going well. But then, in the second week something happened that would stay in my memory forever.

Emma and I were teaching at Baan Gaeyai school on a normal Tuesday morning. During my second lesson of the day, as I was explaining a phrase to my eager - but with the attention span of a goldfish - eight year olds, a loud and deafening bang came from outside, breaking the atmosphere. Suddenly the kids jumped out of their seats and ran out of the classroom onto the balcony outside. As my curiosity had been aroused too, I joined them.

Peering through the hazy, mid-morning sun towards the side road beyond the playing field and the school walls, I could see a car and little else. Wondering what had been the cause of the noise, an educated guess told me there had been a collision of some kind. But, whatever the cause, there was nothing I could do. I had other priorities anyway as the children were excitedly babbling in their native language and not in the slightest bit interested in my lesson any more. I ushered the kids back inside and attempted to rescue the lesson. It wasn't easy but eventually order was restored, though I'm sure they, like me, were still wondering just what had happened. Only at lunchtime did the answer unfold.

June, who came with us every day to help us communicate with the class, as and when we needed it, was chatting to a Thai teacher, obviously discussing what had happened earlier.

"That crash," she said, turning towards us.

"Yes," we replied, puzzled and bewildered.

"Two people have been killed."

I was taken aback and I could tell Emma was too.

"A motorbike overtook a car and went straight into the front of another coming towards the school. Both the men on the bike were killed instantly."

I stared blankly through the dining room window into the school grounds beyond. You don't expect to come to work and this happen. But then I thought about the two victims. Maybe they, only moments earlier, had kissed their parents, wives or girlfriends goodbye – and now they were dead. Apparently the bike rider was drunk. No excuse I know, but who deserves to wake up one morning, get on their bike and die? No one does.

After that, the last lesson of the day proved to be a bit of an anti-climax for myself and Emma. When we arrived home around 2 o'clock we chatted about life being short and how important it is for us all to live it as fully as we can, to grasp every opportunity and not worry about trivial things. Lying down on my bed half an hour later, I plugged my MP3 player into my ears. Turning it on, the song playing was the Scorpions' 'Life is Too Short.' Indeed it is. Listening to the lyrics really emphasised the day's events. That song buzzed around in my head for days afterwards and I knew that, in the future, whenever I heard it, my mind would take me back to that day.

It's almost magical how music can really connect us to moments in our lives. In an instant it transports us back to those good or bad times. It can give us loving inspiration and joy. It can also echo our thoughts and sentiments, depending on the mood we are in when we listen. If that isn't magical, I don't know what is.

***

The day after the King's birthday on the 5th December saw the beginning of our final week. By that time I'd become quite attached to the various groups of children in both schools, so much so that when the last day at Baan Dhaban came, I was not looking forward to saying goodbye. As it turned out, it was a day I won't forget for a long time.

I have to say that I enjoyed teaching in the smaller, compact atmosphere of Baan Dhaban the most. On my final day, I delivered my lesson to my grade 1 class in my trademark style, typically leaping round like some demented keep-fit instructor, getting the children moving and exercising. At the end of the lesson, I turned my back to start packing my bag, ready to move next door to take my next lesson, the grade 2 class. As I turned around, one of the Thai teachers who had spent most of my lessons sitting quietly at the back, helping out when needed, giving instructions in Thai to the class, suddenly and unexpectedly approached me with a gift wrapped in a bag. The class started cheering loudly, and one by one, all stood up and came out in turn, each one handing me a little post-it size card, complete with an outline of a Christmas tree, all individually coloured in by themselves. Each one had a handwritten message, 'To teacher Phil, we hope to meet you again, thank you' or 'To teacher Phil, thank you, you'll be in my memory forever from... unfortunately the whole class had written their names in Thai and I couldn't read them but, as they say, it's the thought that counts and this thought didn't half do that. By the time the last child gave me their carefully written and coloured in card, with the same pride that they must have felt when they created it, a lump appeared in my throat and a tear formed in my eye. I was speechless. Despite my own shortcomings at times during my teaching experience, the rewards and the expressions of gratitude from both the teacher and class were overwhelming. I was more or less reduced to a emotional mess in one easy move. This was a genuine show of appreciation for a volunteer who had given his time, money, passion and commitment in an attempt to improve the language skills of these children.

I began to then think about what I had actually done and how it made me feel. The new T shirt that the children gave me looked quite nice too. That led to posing for photographs with the excited, sad and giddy children whose lives I'd managed to touch and help improve - in such a brief space of time.

My second lesson started about ten minutes later than planned, and the same thing happened after that lesson ended. Finishing off a great and productive lesson, like I'd done so many times with this particular class, I had the kids on their feet, we did some exercises and pronunciation of the grammar we'd learnt, then, as loud as I could, I suddenly shouted;

'Whoa, whoa, whoa', swinging my arms in encouragement.

'Whoa, whoa, whoa', came the almost perfect reply.

'Sweet Child O'Mine' I boldly sang, lifting my hand to my mouth and swinging my arm once more.

'Sweet Child O'Mine' came the enthusiastic and almost perfectly pronounced response.

How priceless was that, especially with a rock classic? And so was the way that they repeated exactly what the grade 1 class had done some sixty minutes earlier, each one giving a handwritten card carrying a message of love and gratitude, each one with a coloured in drawing of a balloon with a teddy bear in the basket. This class were older and their writing was really good, each one carrying the same message of thanks.

'To Phil, we have a good time together, thank you.' From Nitinong, from Peeying, from Tnunya, from Nontasuk, from Napatsorn, in fact from all twenty-four of them. If all the class had been present that day there would have been over thirty coming my way.

At the end of the line came the Thai teacher, handing me a gift. This time I received a Thai silk sarong. Feeling like I'd just won an Oscar or come off stage at some big concert somewhere, I stood at the front of the class, hands on hips and shook my head in disbelief. Moments like this are indeed to be cherished and placed amongst the defining ones that mean the most, ones so rare in everyday life.

By now we had reached lunchtime and Emma told me that she had been given the same reaction and gifts. Not that she needed to tell me; the tear in the corner of her eye did it for her. Before the difficult last lesson we were served a lunch of fantastic Thai cuisine, including red ants which had been made into a soup especially for our last day. I was fast becoming something of a connoisseur in the ant department, having eaten lime flavoured green ants in Australia some years earlier.

Throughout our three weeks together, my grade 3's had been a mixture of either goldfish or, at other times, motivated students. Quite often they cited my frustrations but, at the end of our lesson we arrived at the lesson recap, a game to finish off drilling the learnt language, followed by another favourite chant of mine which I'd taught them; 'No Woman, No Cry' to finish with.

For the third time, at the end of the lesson came the same procession of children, all thirty-five of them patiently waiting to give me their lovely handmade cards featuring a beautifully coloured in drawing of a snowman and Father Christmas, all carrying the same message of love:-

'To teacher Phil, I am feelings happy, I love you.'

I smiled when I saw that message as I did teach them 'feeling happy,' but they just couldn't seem to grasp that one. Again, Parnerecua, Nutthaporn, Nitikarn and the rest of the class had clearly gone to so much effort to reward me for my efforts.

Leaving this classroom was even harder than the previous two, not because the lessons and my volunteering had finished, but the little buggers would not let me go. As I tried to leave the class for our awaiting tuk-tuk, children from every classroom came running towards me and Emma, grabbing our hands, grinning, smiling, shaking our hands, tugging my sweat drenched t-shirt and giving us the widest and biggest smiles imaginable. We left in a whirlwind of waves, smiles, hugs and goodbyes. The journey back home was the quietest, most sombre one there had been over the last three weeks. Neither of us said a word. We couldn't; we were both too choked.

That night Emma and I went out for dinner with June and Adrian and reflected on what an amazing, worthwhile and beneficial experience this introduction to teaching had been. I'll never forget the children's smiles, joy and the appreciation for what I'd tried to give them. The better their English, the better their chance of a brighter future and in my own small way, I had helped them with that. It just made me burst with the sort of personal pride that we experience so few times in our lives.

For me, and for Emma too, the time had passed so quickly and now the time had come for us to part company and move on to the next chapter of our respective journeys. I would be travelling north to Chang Mai before crossing into Laos for Christmas whilst Emma would be heading back to Bangkok to meet up with a friend. We'd become good friends in that short space of time, building up a mutual respect and understanding. Tomorrow I would be on my own again.

***

As my bus pulled up, I thanked Adrian and June for everything they had done over the past three weeks. This had indeed been a fantastic time and I was sad to leave; I'd met some great people, had a fantastic positive experience and, above all, learnt so much from the children of both schools. Once aboard, I settled into my seat and, to soften the blow of leaving, I put on my MP3 player and listened to Metallica. As the bus pulled out of the bus station, destination Chiang Mai, I had a fourteen hour trip ahead of me, plenty of time to reflect and to look forward to the next part of my journey. What could I expect next? After time in Chang Mai, I was going to spend a month exploring Laos, including Christmas and the New Year. I hadn't intended to volunteer again until I reached Cambodia so was looking to have fun and relax instead. After all, since I'd left the UK there had been three projects under my belt - plus the one from Nepal that started it all off. By now, the dark mist and negativity that overshadowed me during the previous twelve months had slowly but surely started to lift, to be replaced with positivity - and it felt good. Mind you, I wasn't relishing having to spend Christmas alone again. But I had wanted to do this trip, so time spent apart from family and friends would be something I would have to accept and deal with. If I could cope with that, what else could I cope with?

***

In Chiang Mai, I hired a moped for a couple of days, swapping the lime green helmet from Ko Lanta for a new, rather awful, bright yellow one. Zipping around a new city, sight-seeing, seemed to be a good way to reflect on what I'd begun to uncover about myself over the past 3 months.

I set off towards Chiang Mai Zoo. In true Farang style, I got lost. Chiang Mai has a rather confusing inner circular road system which, depending on how or where you join it, looks completely the same from every direction. Following the map from my guest-house, which actually bore no resemblance to the road network in place, I joined what I thought was the road heading towards the zoo. Some ten minutes later I was still looking for my exit road when, pulling up at some traffic lights, I happened to lean towards a young lady sat aside her moped waiting patiently for the lights to turn to green.

"Is this the right way to the zoo," I asked her in a rather frustrated tone.

"No," she replied. "But follow me. I can show you."

When the lights changed she turned around and headed in the opposite direction. I followed, weaving in and out of the heavy morning's traffic, trying desperately to keep her in my sights. After what seemed like an age, I pulled up next to her at some traffic lights where there was a sign pointing towards the zoo.

"Thank you very much," I said in the best Thai I could muster, "I can find my way now."

"Okay. Have a good day," she replied.

I thanked her once more and then she turned around and headed back in the direction we had just come from. It suddenly struck me that, without any hesitation, she had not only helped me but had gone completely out of her way to do so. It may seem like a small thing, but it was a simple act of kindness that really touched me. She didn't need to do it, but she did so without any thought.

After parking up at the zoo, I walked around the impressive roads and gardens. Sucking in a lung full of the fresh, mountainous air early on this Monday morning, my journey so far came flooding to the forefront of my mind. Staring into the various enclosures containing brightly coloured birds, their calls offering a soothing background to my thoughts, I started to reflect on what I'd actually achieved in the three months I'd been away from England.

I thought of how I'd had problems and, instead of being sucked into a pit of despair and self pity, I'd overcome them. I thought of how I'd given my time to help others. And then, for some reason, I remembered something a close friend once said to me.

"You can't buy experience" he had told me. "You just pay for it."

I realised now just how right he had been. I'd never fully appreciated before just how simple, yet powerful, that statement was. Our experiences shape us into the people and personalities we become and have an underlying effect on how we try to live our lives. You cannot buy experiences like those I'd had over the past three months, but I did have to give up my time to gain them. Time is one of the most precious gifts we can give as, once it's gone, we can't ever ask for it back. But what a small price to pay for the enrichment it gave me in return. As I thought about this, another far more powerful thought came down on me like a ton of bricks. It was one that had hit me before, in Ko Lanta.

There I had decided that I would not return to my old life. Did I still feel the same way? Damn right I did. After everything I'd done so far, all the planning, the sorting out after the marriage, the gamble I'd taken to leave everything 'safe' behind in order to seek out and find new experiences, new contacts, new friends, maybe a new life, how could I ever return to the mundane existence I'd had in England? Even though I'd previously enjoyed a good standard of living and tried to live my life purposefully, now I was trying to achieve something powerful and introduce lasting changes. So why would I ever stop pursuing that to go back to the civil service I'd been so desperate to pull away from in the first place? Quite simply, I didn't want to. Why should I? If you take yourself off one path to head down another, you wouldn't think about returning to the first path unless, deep down, you knew your choice had been a bad one. And I knew mine had not. I wasn't going down the wrong path; I was trying to be true to myself, to discover what I was truly looking for in my life. Being away from my 'normal' life was not only helping to recharge the batteries, it was getting the creative juices flowing too and hopefully my next move would be down to whatever doors or pathways opened up on the journey ahead.

When I set out on my adventure, I had never intended to change the world. Three months on and I wouldn't be so presumptuous as to say I had – but I knew that the world had changed me.

***

Sitting outside my hotel room in Chiang Mai, I chatted with Brian, a likeable American chap who had been travelling for over three and a half years. He told me he had no intention of ever returning to his old life in the rat race of the city where making money seemed to be more important than living a purposeful life. As we shared stories of what we'd seen and experienced on our travels, together we changed the world in ten easy minutes. We agreed that a simplified existence was needed for everybody in life to benefit from. If the western world was ever going to experience the same kind of riches as its Asian counterparts, materialism and consumerism would need to be outlawed, and friendliness, compassion, honesty and trust brought in by the bucket load. Even gluttony and greed could easily be cured. Thinking of how easy it had been for me to lose 4kg without even trying made me see that, if our diets are so unbalanced maybe that's why so much of our lives are too. We fill them with needless clutter and it shows so much.

***

The remainder of my time in Chiang Mai was, by and large, a very pleasant one. Being up close and personal with tigers is something not many of us would even wish to contemplate but I seized the opportunity to do so at the Tiger Kingdom where, for a small fee of £8, tourists can spend fifteen minutes locked in a cage with up to three of these magnificent beasts. There were, of course, two trainers in there with me. Nonetheless, it was wonderful be able to stroke and truly connect with the animal kingdom in a way we would usually never have the opportunity to do.

I also took a two-day trek, taking in some beautiful ranges north of Chiang Mai and staying overnight at a remote, hill tribe village. The experience of sleeping in a bamboo hut was strange, a bit like sleeping on a trampoline as, whenever someone got up and walked across it, it made everyone else bounce up and down.

It was on this trek that I also became introduced to the card and drinking game elegantly called 'Twat.' Bonding with the eleven other companions over the two days became cemented in spectacular fashion when the majority took part in this rather fun game involving a pack of cards, one less spoon than the number of players, some soot from the pan on the fire, a sense of humour and lots of alcohol.

As a participant loses his hand and fails to collect a spoon, a letter at a time is inscribed in soot onto the unlucky person's forehead. Lose four times and the word 'twat' is spelt, at which point they are out of the game. It showed that random strangers can make strong bonds over something as simplistic as a game of cards. There is and old saying - 'a stranger is a friend I have yet to meet.' Well, strangers very soon become friends when they are writing 'twat' on your forehead.

***

With my sixty day visa about to run out, I left Chiang Mai, ahead of me a fourteen hour overnight bus journey to Vientianne, the capital of Laos. I arrived feeling shell shocked and completely shattered after doing my best 'praying mantis' impression cramped up in the front of the modern, but crammed to the rafters, 12-seater air-conditioned bus. I would look to spend no more than two nights here before making my way up to Vang Vieng a couple of days before Christmas and drop anchor there for the festive period.

On the morning of my second day in Vientianne, whilst having breakfast in a cafe bar, I started thinking: - 'why was I in such a hurry to solve everything there and then?' Over the past week, I'd done a lot of thinking in regards to plans for the future and what my next move would be. Even though I was only three months into the journey, I had started to consider what I would do after the trip came to an end. I thought back to what a fellow traveller had said when this subject had come up in conversation:-

"Just see where the wind blows," was his response.

This kind of resonated with me as my original intention had been, wherever possible, to fly on the 'no plans plan.' But, for some reason, looking for the answer to my future was starting to bug me and I was playing it over and over again in my mind.

As I sipped my coffee, my eardrums busy listening to Europe on my MP3 player, I'd cast my mind back to the end of November when a job that seemed to appear from nowhere arrived in my email inbox. 'Ecoteer' were looking for a Volunteer Co-ordinator. This temporary internship position really caught my eye as it seemed to utilise a lot of the skills I believed I possessed and it was also involved with saving the planet. I'd applied on the off chance. Since then I had heard nothing from them.

Swallowing the fresh coffee, I thought to myself, let's see what happens, after all, the door isn't closed. I'd applied for another volunteer's role teaching English in Cambodia, so what was my sudden rush to find the answers to everything I was looking for? Should I let go of everything, go with the flow, enjoy this new experience and just live for the moment?

Yes, I decided, I should. So, sitting astride my hired complete wreck of a bicycle, I did exactly that. Plugging my MP3 player in, I peddled furiously through the streets and surrounding areas of Vientianne singing out loudly to any local who stared vacantly at me, wondering what I was doing. I enjoyed a mad few hours sightseeing and returned to my guest-house pleasantly tired. Turning on my computer, I checked my email.

There it was in my inbox, an invitation to a Skype interview for the Volunteer Co-ordinators role. In an instant the path I was heading down had grown another fork. Was this the one I was meant to tread down? I didn't know, but it was yet another opportunity.

***

I'd been told not to expect much tarmac in Laos, and I wasn't left disappointed. Quite where the road actually lay beneath all the dust and potholes I doubt anyone knew. The three and a half hour journey from Vientianne was bumpy, to say the least. If the bus hit one pothole, it must have hit a hundred. Still, the scenery was stunning and the sight of the mountains against a beautiful pure blue sky greeted us as we approached Vang Vieng, although I wasn't sure just how much of the bus would be left by the time it actually got there.

Vang Vieng itself is essentially a party town, only springing into life around fifteen years ago. Wherever you walk through the streets there are scores of backpacker hostels, guesthouses and bars. It resembles a 'wild west' kind of place with dusty streets and broken, unfinished buildings but there is undoubtedly some charm to the town.

The same can be said of the people too. Leaving my guesthouse to visit the shop opposite, the shopkeeper beckoned me to join him and two friends to enjoy a beer. This had happened in Vientianne too. How nice it was to be invited for a beer with the locals with nothing expected in return except a genuine interest in where I was from and why I was travelling in Laos. Here again I saw the kindness of South East Asian people shining through. They were only too happy to spend time with me and, of course, practise their English at the same time.

***

Thinking back to the same time last year, I concentrated on how my Christmas had been a rather flat, emotional time with my head in another dimension, trying to make sense of what had happened and what would happen in the future. I had really done something amazing with my life in the time since. I'd brought compassion and humanity to more people than I ever thought I would. I had also begun the first very important steps of trying to change and make my life something much more than it had been. The seeds of my future were now being sown. I was starting to design my life, one that would hopefully suit my needs. How would it feel if we all could design and build our perfect life? As I experienced more and more new wonders, the choices were indeed beginning to unfold and present themselves as new opportunities to take a different pathway.

I was on my own now though. But what a year I'd had. I'd started to turn a dire situation into one that was changing my life in a positive way. The pain had almost healed, even though the memories still remained. In all honesty, they always would but, in less than twelve months, I had taken massive leaps forward. I had sorted all the marriage related issues out and, more importantly, begun this journey of self-discovery. I had completed four charitable projects, each one different and each one offering a fresh perspective on life. I was re-taking control and it felt good, powerful even, and do you know what? I was proud. Very proud. I also had an interview for a job lined up, experienced countries and cultures unchartered for me beforehand, and had seen some beautiful, stunning natural beauty along the way.

Three months into this trip and I was well on the way to achieving something. I had met some great, positive people, helped mankind and touched other people's lives in some way, shape or form.

All this positive thinking was hiding the fact that I was missing family and friends. So, what did I do to help alleviate the situation? I dealt with it head on. I went caving, kayaking, mountain biking and took a hot air balloon trip through the gorgeous mountain valley. Jumping onto a rubber tube on a trip one day, I even followed a Frenchman wearing only a pair of 'budgie smugglers' into a river cave. How frightening was that? And four days later, on Christmas Day, when last year's memory reminded me of a twelve hour shift in a place I didn't want to be - face first into a vodka bottle floating on a river of pain, despair and frustration - I was now, a million miles away from that dark place, floating into somewhere completely different and unexpected...

7
Buckets, Bad Guts and a New Year

It was one o'clock in the afternoon on Christmas Day and I was standing in the river front 'Q Bar,' in Vang Vieng, Laos. In my right hand I was clutching a plastic bucket containing whisky, pineapple juice and red bull. Only a minute or two before that, I had been holding a large rubber inner tube. I was in a place so far removed from the same time the year before, it felt almost surreal.

I'd met some great people in my guest house who had dragged me here, not quite kicking and screaming, to help make it a Christmas Day to remember. That is how I came to be spending it floating down the Nam Song River to the accompaniment of dance music loud enough to shatter glasses – probably the reason we were drinking out of buckets. It wasn't only loud, it was bloody awful too. I much prefer Iron Maiden, Metallica, Europe or any rock/metal music in general. Even so, as I shared a bucket with two others at the Q bar, I was determined to make the most of the situation.

The sun was beating down so strongly, if it hadn't been for my cap the bloody thing would have fried my brain. I didn't need it to do that as buckets of rapidly disappearing whisky, red bull and pineapple juice were already frying it from the inside. As I glanced around the bar through an alcoholic haze, I started to feel like Will Ferrell's character 'Frank the Tank' from the cult film 'Old School.' Trying to compete with groups of girls and guys, most of whom were barely half my age, I felt like the oldest swinger in town. As I stood there trying to look as cool as anyone dressed in only board shorts, singlet, shades and sandals could, doing my best to ignore the crappy, repetitive dance tune attacking my eardrums, I smiled and thought, 'I really don't care.' For once in my life I was literally living on the 'no plans plan.' I didn't have a clue how long that would continue but not only did it feel really good, it felt so liberating too.

So here I was, 'tubing,' the term given to floating in a rubber tube from bar to bar on a two mile or so stretch of the river, getting as pissed as a fart along the way, drinking the contents of as many buckets as my liver could handle between now and around 6 o'clock in the evening when it would be a case of float down to the finish or stagger back into town, minus my tube and 60,000 kip deposit. And then the assault on my liver would continue, drinking well into the night. That wasn't quite what I intended, but I was determined to enjoy myself and see what happened.

Standing there, looking around at the scantily clad young girls and groups of young lads thinking they had landed in heaven, I remembered how I started the beginning of this year. Back then I couldn't even have imagined being here, of all places. 'I deserved this' I thought. Four hours of acting like a complete fool, throwing myself off zip lines and platforms or floating down the river in a tractor tyre tube seemed almost too surreal to imagine, but hell, what fun it was. I don't remember making it past bar number 5 and, without a tyre for company, I lost my deposit, but a great party all the same. Every year there are usually at least seven fatalities here as people get so fucked up, they either drown or smash their heads on the rocks – quite common if the level of the river is low. You have to remember that 'health and safety' doesn't exist out here; you have to rely on your own common sense and personal responsibility to watch what you are doing. Unfortunately when one takes excessive amounts of alcohol on board, common sense usually abandons ship, so it's easy to get carried away. Perhaps I should have understood the risks more because I was older. Even so, for once, I didn't act my age; I acted like a total twat, doing every swing, jump and slide. By the end of the night I fell exhausted into a drunken slumber ready to... yes, you guessed it, do the same again on Boxing Day.

After awakening on Boxing Day with a head as thick as a brick, I again duly collected a tube and headed back to the river to act like a teenager for one last time before leaving for Luang Prabang. Not being in a rush to start drinking again, I nursed the first beer like it was the last one I would ever drink. Slowly, my stomach and head returned to something like normal and, after a more chilled day this time, I decided to meet up with James, one of the chaps from my guest house, for a farewell beer before we went our separate ways the following day.

***

Since leaving England, I had been pleasantly surprised by how the people I had encountered, locals, volunteers and fellow travellers, had all been wonderful. Humanity and compassion had rated highly and not once had I felt threatened, unsafe or at risk. But what I witnessed on my final night here in Vang Vieng made me so angry it almost completely destroyed my faith in humanity.

After a couple of drinks with James, I crossed a rickety old bridge to the Sunset and Bucket bars. Sometime later, with my liver in danger of meltdown, I decided that enough was enough and headed back to the guest house. As I approached the bridge, up ahead three or four guys appeared from nowhere and were searching tourists heading towards the bars. I spotted James and acknowledged him just as one of these 'Tourist Police' chaps proceeded to give him a search. As he was given probably the worst rub down search I have ever seen, this guy suddenly pulled what looked like tissue from his hand and then pretended to have removed it from James's pocket. As he asked James what it was, a look of both surprise and shock washed across his face.

There is a burgeoning drugs scene within Laos which the authorities are aware of. Every now and again the Tourist Police pretend that they are actually concerned about it and try to clamp down on it – which they apparently do by stitching up innocent victims.

James was taken to the police station where they punched him, slammed his head into the table and asked him where he had got the 'drugs' - which actually looked like bits of twigs. They then brought him back to our guest house and confiscated his passport before returning to the police station to continue their 'interrogation.'

Feeling a duty of concern after finding out that they were taking him off to the Tourist Police Station, I headed off to see if I could help him in some way. The trouble is though, once you have had a few drinks, things aren't as clear as they should be. Besides, there was little I could do. After all, if they could 'frame' the totally innocent James, what was there to stop them doing the same to me?

The police eventually gave James back the contents of his pockets and he was released, under the proviso that he report back at eight thirty the next morning. When he did so, he was told he would be 'fined' 5 million kip - about £390 - for his 'drug possession.' This scam technique in Laos's corrupt infra-structure had claimed its latest victim. In a country where the average yearly income is $1000, these 'gentlemen' conduct their 'business' as a way of supplementing their meagre income.

After letting James sweat until only twenty-five minutes before he was due to leave for Bangkok, the fine was suddenly reduced to three and a half million kip - around £275 - no doubt to go straight into the back pockets of these people. He had been stitched up like a kipper and didn't have any choice other than to pay the bribe - or run the risk of being put in a Laos prison. One thing I hate is corrupt authorities. I'd hoped that I wouldn't be caught up in anything like this, and really felt for James.

Just imagine if this happened to you? How would you deal with it? I did worry about it as I was travelling independently. It certainly left a sour taste in the mouth as I said my goodbyes and boarded my bus for the trip to the old capital of Luang Prabang.

***

On the five and a half hour journey north I sat next to Blayur, a likeable Canadian who taught English in Japan. We chatted about anything and everything, putting both our respective worlds to right as we endured the precarious journey on a typically bad Laos road. Travelling on long journeys is so much better when people like Blayur are on board, people to connect with and enjoy their company. Travelling alone is fantastic for the soul in so many ways and meeting new people is one of the most enjoyable parts of the experience. You never know who you may bump into and what they could potentially offer you. In most cases though, it's nothing more than a pleasant chat in good company.

Over the next few days, in the beautiful French colonial city of Luang Prabang, I took time out to relax. I rode a mountain bike, socialised, drank nice beer, ate locally on the market... and became ill. I should have known better than to eat meat from the markets. When walking past the cluttered stalls, the sight of carcasses hanging on rusty hooks or chickens' feet and heads presented on platters were enough to make anyone sick. But, when travelling, I have always adopted the 'when in Rome' outlook, immersing myself in the local culture and sampling local food. Sometimes though it can be like playing Russian roulette with your digestive system and this was one occasion when I lost, being struck down with sickness and diarrhoea.

***

On New Year's Eve, as the beautiful sight of thousands of

Chinese Lanterns were lit and floated off into a clear fresh New Years' night, I stared up and reflected on this past year, of how I'd found the strength to move forward and how I'd met so many wonderful, beautiful people. As the lanterns rose higher and higher and many more new ones were released beginning their journeys into the night sky, I felt happy and content with my own progress but, like the lanterns, not quite sure where I would be floating to next. I gazed into the sky admiring their beauty, listening to the sounds of happy people shouting and celebrating the beginning of a New Year. Even though I wanted to be with them, I wasn't. As the shouts from the crowded bars grew louder, as the clocks struck midnight, I was running around the back to be sick.

By the following morning however, I had started to feel better, and having by now parted company with Blayur, I had began to plot out the first leg of the New Year travels. I'd heard nothing about the volunteer co-ordinator job that I'd had an interview for just before Christmas, so now seemed like the ideal time to plan my next volunteer project. I would be going to Cambodia next and intended to look for one there. Before that though, I decided to head up to the town of Houay Xai on the Thai / Laos border to try my hand at zip lining on the 'Gibbon Experience.'

Climbing aboard the 'VIP' bus that evening, I settled into my cramped and rather hot seat, preparing for the fourteen hour journey to take me north as far as the border. I had already booked a flight five days later to Pakse, planning to hit the Four Thousand Islands before crossing the border into Cambodia, so this would hopefully be a fun way to round up my time in Laos. Public Transport in Laos is generally not very good. I was charged 200,000 kip for the 'privilege' of waiting an additional two hours before taking my seat on a 'VIP' bus for nigh on fifteen hours with hardly room to breathe. The bus company had overfilled the bus, even putting a row of plastic chairs down the aisle, leaving us 'falangs' crammed into any available space. For the entire journey I had to suffer the smell of the locals' breath which even seemed to find its way into my ears and down my neck. Eventually, after a hazardous and perilous journey, the bus rolled into Houay Xai around 09.45. I and two kiwi girls, fellow sufferers from the bus, jumped into a waiting Hilux to take us into the jungle and the Gibbon Experience.

***

As I climbed higher and higher into the canopies of the Bokeo Nature Reserve jungle, sweat poured from me like a dripping tap. Carrying a day-pack ready for the overnight stay in a tree house 300 feet up from the jungle floor, the heat of the mid morning sun showed no mercy. The two litres of water I was carrying quickly disappeared as I desperately attempted to rehydrate my body. Eventually though we stopped climbing and our guide led us to the start of the zip lines.

After the 'safety briefing' of very broken grunts interspersed with the occasional English word and a quick visual demonstration of how to attach both the runner and the safety rope to the zip line, we were left to trust in an inch thick piece of cable stretching four hundred metres across the forest, and around four hundred feet above its floor on the first of around twenty-five zip lines we would tackle that day. Not having had the opportunity to try anything like this before, I put my faith and trust in the 'one above' as I started to slide away from the safety of the forest floor on the first zip line. As the floor below vanished, air took its place and the adrenaline rush that followed was up there with the very best experiences in life. Being suspended so far up, with so little means of support, was exhilarating. If that one little wire were to snap, there would be no walking away from that one. As the day unfolded, each zip line was treated with the same respect but with a growing sense of anticipation and expectation.

When the day came to an end we were left to stay overnight in the tree house some three hundred feet above the forest floor. There I took a shower with one of the most amazing views high above the forest, where the monkeys and the rest of the jungle population could witness me in all my glory. Not that there was any need for privacy up here, except of course from the eight other guests. That night, the nine of us bonded over a game of cards and an awful bottle of wine.

By the end of day two, four of us had booked to set sail the following day down the Mekong river to Luang Prabang. The slow boat gave a fantastic opportunity to see Laos from a river aspect, watching the world go by with the Laos people on one side and Thai's on the other, all going about their daily business. After thoroughly enjoying the two days it took to travel, I again reached Luang Prabang before flying to Pakse and catching a local bus down to the Four Thousand Islands near to the Cambodian border.

The countryside there is really quite beautiful, and seizing the opportunity to hire a push bike and cycle along the islands of Don Det and Don Khon, my time there proved to be quite inspirational in more ways than one. Admiring the vast open fields and struggling to keep my balance on its rugged, narrow tracks, I'd plugged in my MP3 player and set off for a tour of the islands. Not having noticed someone else on the path, I swerved suddenly to avoid a chap heading towards me. We exchanged greetings and, as I could tell that he wanted to talk further, I pulled over. Introducing himself as Adrian Robson from Bridlington, we swapped stories of travelling until he reached into his rucksack and pulled out a copy of his book:- 'South-east Asia, In yer Face.' Interesting, I thought, or coincidence, as he started to tell his tale of how, in November 2003 he was caught up in the flooding of the Bahorok river in Bukit Lawang, Sumatra, Indonesia. He was one of few survivors of a disaster that claimed over 239 lives, with around 1400 locals also losing their homes, as 400 houses, 3 mosques, 8 bridges, 280 kiosks, and 35 hotels and guest houses were destroyed. After constantly asking himself 'Why me and not them?' he'd resigned himself to dying more than once that day and, eight years later, still struggled to understand why he had lived and so many had died.

I stood there in amazement as his story unfolded. Two months after his brush with death, he suddenly felt compelled to write his experiences into a book. That sounded familiar, I thought. His was a really interesting story and one that deserved to be told. He went on to say that, after endless knock backs from publishers wanting to change his experiences into someone else's words, he decided to photocopy his work and has spent the last six years selling it at every opportunity. So far he had sold over 5,600 copies. What an inspiring guy and story. What he must have gone through that day is hard to imagine but witnessing carnage and pain in that way must have affected him deeply. Imagine being caught up in that? It certainly made me think how lucky most of us are and also how our lives can end as quickly as they began.

His was a story that really connected with me. Although I hadn't stared death in the face, I'd had an experience that had disrupted my life so much that I too had the overwhelming urge to write. It had been one hell of a coincidence to randomly bump into someone who shared that urge, to write about his personal experiences as a way of helping others. Adrian told me that, after he had written his thirty thousand words, the urge left him as quickly as it had appeared and he has written nothing since.

***

I spent the remainder of my time chasing the difficult to spot - and decreasing in numbers - Irrawaddy dolphins around the Four Thousand Islands in a kayak; a great way to pass the time before embarking on yet another fourteen hour bus journey, this time to Siem Reap in Cambodia.

There I had managed to find another volunteering opportunity at the 'Cambodian Children's House of Peace.' After spending the last four weeks relaxing and sightseeing, I felt relieved that once again, more purpose would be added to my trip. As I waited for my bus I found myself chatting with a Finnish couple who seemed quite surprised when I told them what I was doing. When you do get feedback or compliments, it does help spur you on in many ways. Travelling can, and does, get very lonely; to hear words of encouragement from complete strangers can stop you disappearing into yourself at the times when dark thoughts cloud over you, times when your thoughts start to drift back to loved ones back home or times when the enormity of what you are doing and where you are really hit home. Their words certainly provided another moment of much needed strength to draw from, so much so that, as the bus crossed the border into Cambodia, I started to feel more upbeat. By now I was more confident in talking to anyone, though just as happy in my own company. I looked at my expectations for Cambodia and with a new project lined up, they looked good. I was looking forward to spending time around the temples of Angkor Wat and Siem Reap but I still thought deeply about the possibility of new openings coming from this trip.

So far I'd done three charity projects and, even though they were all unique and inspiring, no new openings had come off the back of them. So, by the next morning, the wave of optimism had been replaced by one of loneliness, frustration and fear about the possibility of having to return to my old life back in England. Three weeks had passed since I had an interview for the Volunteer Co-ordinator job in Malaysia and as I hadn't heard whether I was successful or not, it was now bugging me.

No matter how I tried to think positively, I couldn't shift my mood and it dropped further as I surveyed my possibilities. For the first time in the nearly four months of being away, for some inexplicable reason, I really felt like throwing in the towel and booking the next flight home. To make matters worse, that night I unexpectedly came down with chronic diarrhoea again, the third time in as many weeks.

The next day, after a dreadful night's sleep, constantly being woken at all hours with terrible stomach cramps and an urge to use the toilet, I cried. I lay in bed, thought of everything, my family, my friends, my future and what I was doing on this trip. I didn't know what to think but travelling alone and, feeling the need for companionship, I felt like it was all too much. It was starting to burn deep and take its toll on me. As I lay on the bed rubbing my stomach and gazing up at the ceiling, I started to wonder, 'how was I going to get out of this one?

8
Beauty and the Beast

Cambodia is certainly steeped in history. From the origins of the great Angkor Wat and its fascinating temples through to the brutal, harsh civil war and the resulting Khmer Rouge dictatorship from 1975 till 1979, it is a country that has seen some truly testing and challenging times. Hundreds of thousands of Cambodians lost their lives at the hands of Pol Pot's enforced regime and hundreds of thousands more perished from famine, dysentery and starvation. More than a fifth of the country's population of eight million were systematically wiped out. It's hard to imagine that this went on only a short time ago, but it did and it was kept virtually secret from the outside world at the time. Now, that is disturbing enough in itself but imagine how the Cambodian people must have felt being powerless to prevent Pol Pot from carrying out his Agrarian Socialist Revolution and destroying anyone and everything that got in his path.

After spending two days sorting my head and rear end out, then a further two days temple spotting at the quite magnificent Angkor Wat, in utter awe of the way these temples came to be here, I was now keen to get involved with The Cambodian Children's House of Peace where I had arranged to teach English.

Home to seventeen girls and fifteen boys, most of the children here are either orphans or have come from such poor families that their parents simply cannot afford to bring them up. The centre takes them in and looks after them. Its core philosophy is to provide a decent moral upbringing and a good education, along with opportunities as they get older to gain work placements or apprenticeships, either in Cambodia or with sponsors from abroad.

Gaining qualifications and employment would give them the best possible start they could wish for and learning English is a vital part of their future. What they learn from volunteers is often the only way they can be exposed to native speakers. Other than that their only exposure to English is from Khmer teachers reading out of an English book.

Arriving at the centre on my first day of teaching, I liked the place straight away. It was not too dissimilar from what I'd experienced in the children's home in Nepal. From the conditions and the upkeep it was evident that no government money was being directed at it. The centre relied on sponsors and donations from around the world to make this a sanctuary of love and peace. Also known in Khmer as Santepheap, meaning peace, it is a place that its founder members would be proud to see.

The first thing that hit me as I walked around the dusty, bare grounds was how happy, friendly and warm all the children were. They were utterly compelling, polite, respectful and a pleasure to interact with. This made me want to get involved as much as I could. Not only did they want to learn, they wanted to have fun at the same time. I met up with two other volunteers, David and James and, without a curriculum to follow, we looked at what had been taught the previous week and together we made up a lesson plan for the day, one suitable for both morning and afternoon classes. No class size reached over twelve which meant that I could get really involved in a more personal way of teaching, suiting my teaching style perfectly.

It literally was a joy, with the children keen to learn and surprising me with just how good their knowledge of English was. Lessons were fun, informative and personal, given that there were nearly as many teachers as students. But that didn't matter; it made the whole experience worth more. Materials and resources were scarce and it meant more thinking on one's feet and finding other ways to structure a class, but wasn't that part of the fun? By the end of the first day I knew that what I'd learnt about teaching in Thailand had stayed with me and I felt confident to be able to help these kids the best that I could.

At the end of my first day at the orphanage I'd cycled the two kilometres from the school to Angkor Wat, to use up the last day of my $40 three day temple pass. Cycling was a great way to see and appreciate the sheer beauty of this magical, spiritual place for one last time. As I furiously peddled my six-speed machine around the Big Circle, the larger loop of temples that circled around the main Angkor Wat temple, my mind suddenly travelled back to late October and the game of pool in Ko Lanta I'd had with Ross when the Camino de Santiago had come up in conversation.

As I marvelled at this serene, mysterious place, the idea suddenly came to me that, even though I had already decided I would do it a month or two after my return to England, I would now do it for a charity. What a great idea I thought. Not only would I benefit from achieving something amazing but so would a worthy cause - and the one which would benefit seemed very clear to me.

Bury Hospice provides end of life and palliative care for terminally ill patients and support for their families. With family and friends already connected to working there, it felt right somehow. None of the other charities I'd volunteered for so far were personal, but this one sort of was. I'd also thought of selling up in Yorkshire and returning to my home-town of Bury, so it all seemed to link in quite nicely. As the idea developed and spun wildly around in my head, I even thought of the name for the trip:- 'Boots, Beer & Bury Hospice.' This summed up my love of walking, beer and of course charity. I was impressed with that one. As the idea unfolded more, I began to see myself in my mind's eye not only walking the walk but also the posters I could create to promote it. Whether that meant the idea was a good one or that it was just meant to be, I didn't know. Either way I just knew that I would put this together when I returned to the UK.

As the week at the school progressed, I started to learn more things about myself. The class numbers here varied from around seven to twelve, depending on whether the children went to school in the morning or afternoon – with those not attending studying English with the volunteers at the home. I was really surprised, yet so pleased, how enthusiastic they were to learn English. For the week I was there I found it an absolute pleasure to teach them. Lessons were fun, yet they worked hard. The age range was between 8 and 15. Regardless of ability they all worked together to help each other and were more than keen to practice their new words and sentences. Teaching these boys and girls I learnt more patience than I did in Surin, where I had found myself frustrated with the class sizes and the constant battle to keep so many entertained at once. Here I could spend more time with each student and, by having this luxury, found that the results were more forthcoming. I was enjoying the experience of volunteering once again.

Sitting in my hostel one night, I suddenly wondered how else I could help the children. Remembering the kindness from the children in Surin, I looked in my rucksack and found the gifts of a sarong, T shirt, and silk shawl they'd given me when I finished at the school. Rummaging further I found another T shirt and some medical supplies I didn't need. On my last day at the house I gave them all to the orphanage. Looking at my needs and theirs, there was no argument really. My small donation of clothes and medical supplies, along with the week of my time I'd readily given, would go further than I imagined it would. Kindness and humility goes such a long way and these children had so much of both, along with so many of the other basic values they were being taught by the centre. I wished I could have helped in many other ways too. They were so thankful of anything and everything they were given, had impeccable manners, they gave thanks before every meal and always ate together. They deserved whatever came their way, and in the week I was there they had earned everything by the bucket load and it was truly a pleasure to have shared that with them.

Imagine how children in the western world would benefit from a learning experience like this? Imagine them spending a week with no I-phones, computer games or TV, having to sleep on the floor, share each other's clothes, take cold showers, wash their clothes by hand, cook over an open fire and being constantly attacked by flies, mosquitoes and anything else that moved?

How these children appreciated and valued everything they had and the way they helped each other made me feel very humble and think about things back home more deeply. It gave me so much more appreciation of what we cast aside as not being important anymore. How wrong we are.

Leaving Siem Reap, heading for Phnom Penh, I looked back on the last 10 days. At the beginning I had suffered another blip and lack of direction but, from the positive experience of The Cambodian Children's House of Peace, now felt back on track. I had decided to keep travelling and still look for new volunteer opportunities whilst doing so. I had joined 'Workaway,' another purposeful travel website, which would give access to new and different volunteer projects. I knew that once again I could move onwards with renewed confidence and a warm feeling inside, gleaned from the teaching experience.

I now wanted to see the Killing Fields and Tuol Sleng detention centre in Phnom Penh to learn more about events in recent Cambodian history. Every time I turned a corner the devastating effects on the country were evident so I knew that this would be upsetting to see. Quite how I would feel after I'd seen them, I didn't know.

Travelling on an overnight bus with a great Canadian couple I'd met back in Houay Xai, together we visited Choeung Ek Genocide Centre, around 15 km from Phnom Penh and one of the three hundred or so Killing Fields dotted around Cambodia from the Khmer Rouge regime.

Beginning on the 17th April 1975, Pol Pot's army descended

into Phnom Penh. Within three days they had completely wiped out its infrastructure, forcing everyone into the countryside to begin his twisted idea of an Agrarian Socialist Revolution, condemning anyone he looked upon as an enemy of the state to certain death in Tuol Sleng Prison, here at Choeung Ek or the other Killing Fields that began to spring up around Cambodia. Under the reign of Pol Pot's Khmer Rouge, an estimated two and a half million people were estimated to have died.

Over seventeen thousand men, women and children were executed and murdered here in ways too cruel to imagine. In this killing field alone, over a hundred and twenty-nine mass graves were unearthed, some holding up to four hundred bodies, a total of around 8,895 victims. As I silently drifted through the site, listening to the audio commentary on the headset, I tried to imagine what it might have been like to have come to a place like this back in the late 70's. Now a place of peace and serenity, listening to the horrors unfold from survivors whilst walking around could only give a partial insight into what the suffering of every poor unfortunate soul who passed through these gates might have been like. Arriving from Tuol Sleng - also known as S-21 interrogation and detention centre - in cattle trucks in the middle of the night, the poor victims would be led blindfolded to the edge of a mass grave and then killed in unspeakable ways, their bodies dumped into mass graves.

By the time I reached the 'killing tree' where children were brutally snatched from their mothers' arms, swung by the feet into the tree and murdered while they were forced to watch, I really wanted to cry but the tears wouldn't come. I could feel the oppression, the pain and the suffering with every step I took in this place. It wasn't a nice feeling, but how it made me think. The mental images became firmly etched into my mind and were not going anywhere any time soon.

Three hours later I arrived at the gates of Tuol Sleng, formerly the primary and high school, Chao Ponhea, before it became a detention and interrogation centre for the Khmer Rouge. There are five main school buildings here and each one served a different purpose. People were herded like cattle and imprisoned in crudely built cells, treated without dignity or humanity, more often than not tortured and then transported to their deaths.

Over 17,000 people were thought to have been imprisoned here. Upon arrival at the prison, prisoners were photographed and required to talk about their lives, beginning with their childhood and ending with their arrest. After that, they were forced to strip to their underwear and their possessions were confiscated. The prisoners were then taken to their cells. Those taken to the smaller cells were shackled to the walls or the concrete floor. Those who were held in the large mass cells were shackled to long pieces of iron bar and slept on the floor without mats, mosquito nets, or blankets. They were forbidden to talk to each other.

The day in the prison began at 4:30 a.m. when prisoners were stripped and checked to see if their shackles were loose or if the prisoners had hidden objects they could use to commit suicide. Over the years, several prisoners managed to kill themselves, so the guards were very careful in checking the shackles and cells. The prisoners received four small spoonfuls of rice porridge and a watery soup of leaves twice a day. Drinking water without asking the guards for permission resulted in serious beatings. The inmates were hosed down every four days.

The prison had very strict regulations and severe beatings were handed out to any prisoner who tried to disobey. Almost every action had to be approved by one of the prison's guards. Prisoners were sometimes forced to eat human faeces and drink human urine. The unhygienic living conditions in the prison caused skin diseases, lice, rashes, ringworm and other nasty complaints. The prison's medical staff were untrained and offered treatment only to sustain prisoners' lives when they had been injured during interrogation. When prisoners were taken from one place to another for interrogation, their faces were covered. Guards and prisoners were not allowed to talk to each other and people who were in different groups were not allowed to have contact with one another.

Can you imagine what that must have been like for every poor soul that came through the gates? Most prisoners at S-21 were held for two to three months. Within two or three days of their arrival, all prisoners were taken for interrogation. The torture system at Tuol Sleng was designed to make prisoners confess to whatever crimes they were charged with by their captors. Prisoners were routinely beaten and tortured with electric shocks, hot metal instruments and hanging, as well as through the use of various other devices. Some prisoners were cut with knives, suffocated with plastic bags or had their fingernails pulled out. Sometimes prisoners' heads were held under water and waterboarding was also used. Only seven survivors emerged from here when it was liberated in early 1979. How this was allowed to happen, no one can imagine, but it did. We should never forget every poor innocent victim of this dictator and his Marxist regime. The country, with the spirit of its people trying hard to rebuild it, is slowly recovering. Only time will continue to develop this beautiful country and educate every visitor who comes to see the horrors of what war can bring. The Cambodian people are probably some of the nicest that I have experienced across Asia. Ignoring the persistent annoyance of tuk tuk drivers, or the offer of drugs or 'boom boom', the people are without doubt some of the most genuine and friendliest in all of South East Asia. They desperately welcome the tourist boom that ironically exists as a direct result of the atrocities.

Throughout Cambodia, landmines left over from the turbulent past still claim 6-700 victims every year. Travelling through the country, the number of legless, armless, or blinded victims is upsetting to see. If I could, I would readily give to every single one I saw, but the reality is that you can't. You can only help those that you can. Maybe it's better to try and focus help on a minority and do it well rather than throwing a dollar at every man, woman or child lying in the street. I prefer to volunteer in one place at a time, but we can all help in so many different ways. Any way helps, but why does man have to treat its fellow man like this? Cambodia opens so many treasures to its visitors and it is a growing and developing country yet there is no infrastructure in place to help the unfortunate victims of war or poverty. In Phnom Penh especially, the number of NGO's driving Hilux's or other unnecessarily large and expensive vehicles is shocking. Even though in their own way they are trying to help, maybe not rubbing people's noses into the ground and spending donations and money thrown their way on smaller cars may help those that truly need it. Will that ever be the case though?

After relaxing in the little fishing village of Kep, 173kms south west from the capital, Kampot was the next place on the list of Cambodian places to visit and, sailing down the Kampot River in this quaint old colonial town a few days later, I looked at a young couple as they sat across from me on the boat. Obviously in love, the way they gazed longingly into each other's eyes made me wonder if I'd ever find true love again. I wasn't jealous of what they had, after all I'd had it too, then lost it - but I couldn't help thinking that after more than twelve months of being on my own, would my princess come knocking on my door once more - or was I to forever walk the earth alone? Either way, I knew that looking for love was not the answer, however hard it might be. In life, things turn up when you least expect them to. I, and probably many others, know that love is exactly like that. Trust and have faith and don't worry about it, I told myself, and keep moving forwards alone with the hope and belief that things will work out. Who knows what the future holds?

Chatting to an elderly Scottish chap in a local bar after watching some much needed English football on TV, the same topic came up in conversation, with him mentioning how he met his wife. It will come I know it will, I thought, I have to accept that in life there are things we cannot order, love being one. It walks in when we least expect it. Maybe it won't happen for me on this trip but at least I've moved out of my comfort zone; I was challenging myself in many other ways and having an amazing experience at the same time.

Hitting the lively seaside town of Sihanoukville, I only had around ten days of my visa left and I wanted to see whatever else I could of this vastly developing country. A week relaxing on a beach seemed to be the best medicine. In Cambodia's premier beach-side resort there is no shortage of annoyance from the tuk-tuk or moto drivers. By this time though, quite against my own morals, I had started to ignore them. I felt quite guilty about this at first, until I realised that it is the only way to deal with being repeatedly asked if you require their services.

Planning the next stage of the trip was now coming together nicely. I'd planned to visit New Zealand in January 2011 but after it was cancelled and I began planning this trip, I'd decided that it was one place that had to go on my itinerary not only because I desperately wanted to visit this amazing place, but also because it would help to lay the ghost of my marriage split to rest. Hopefully, it would also allow me to look for new volunteer opportunities whilst there. With a place to stay in Christchurch with Julia, a volunteer I'd met at Lanta Animal Welfare, the starting point for exploring New Zealand was now on the map. Arranging the flights, I would head back overland to Bangkok for a few days before flying to Hanoi in Vietnam. There I would see Sapa and Halong Bay for a week, fly to Ho Chi Minh City and from there take a direct flight to New Zealand.

Excited at the prospect of now finally visiting and spending time in the country I had dreamed of seeing for many years, I decided to do nothing for the remainder of my 30 day visa except stay in Sihanoukville and head off to the island of Koh Rong and put myself into seclusion with not much more than nature for company. I could recharge the batteries and, with replies from Workaway now appearing in my inbox, a rough plan had started to appear about spending my time in New Zealand constructively.

There was however one final thing that I was to do before I

went to the island and, quite by chance, as is normally the way these things usually work, that piece came together when I least expected it to.

9
This is Gonna Hurt!

Looking at the free coastal guide in Kampot, an advert for a tattooist in Sihanoukville caught my eye. As a tattoo virgin, I'd always fancied having one done but, whenever I'd looked into it before, I couldn't find the right design or the right tattooist. Scrolling through the pages of Sinville Tattoo's website, I was instantly impressed by Mark's work and his obvious passion for tattooing. Mark, a British tattoo artist, works in Cambodia for nine months of the year, affording him a simpler and cheaper existence than in the UK.

I was drawn to his honest profile page, his striking designs and artwork. Could this be the man for the job? Hmmm. As for a tattoo, I always knew that I wanted a lion of some description. My birth sign is Leo and in many ways it symbolised my character and persona. But, more to the point, to me it was symbolic of what I'd overcome so far. Perhaps too it would give me the spiritual and mental strength I needed to move forward to the next stage of my life. That may sound silly but isn't that why so many of us get tattoos, to symbolise something in our lives? For me this wasn't any different. I was quite excited at the prospect and thought that, at my age, I must not have any regrets about whatever I choose to have permanently etched into my skin.

The next day I left Kampot and headed for Sihanoukville with Mark's tattoo parlour on my 'to visit as soon as I arrived' list. It turned out quite strange really. The day I arrived I decided to pay him a visit and see whether he would be able to fit me in for a tattoo whilst I was there. Cycling past his shop on my hired mountain bike, I saw he was busy chatting to a customer, so I carried on, intending to return some other time. But, as I sped down the hill and turned the corner at the foot of the hill, there, quite by chance, stood a magnificent pair of lion statues, proudly guarding the entrance to a big hotel.

I stopped my bike, suddenly exclaiming; 'That's it!' Finally after years of searching, quite by chance I had finally seen the source of inspiration for my tattoo. Excitedly, I turned round and made my way back up to the shop and explained to Mark what I'd seen. As he could fit me in on the 6th February, the day before I was due to leave, I made an appointment with him to discuss my idea further.

Strange isn't it, how things seemed to be effortlessly fitting together?

Together we looked at photographs I'd taken and we found ones that Mark would be able to turn into a great tattoo. Giving him full design freedom, I left the rest to him to make the transfer that would form the base of my tattoo.

***

Things really seemed to be coming together now. The flights to Hanoi in North Vietnam, from there to Ho Chi Minh City and then to Christchurch, New Zealand were cast in a tablets of stone. Add to that an email I'd received from a project on the 'Workaway' website, wanting my help with carpentry and joinery at a Holiday Park in New Zealand's South Island, I felt really elated. I realised that, by being positive and pro-active in looking for new ventures and projects, doors were beginning to open and now it seemed, several were doing so at the same time. After feeling ready to pack it all in just three short weeks earlier, my inner strength was growing again as the pieces in this jigsaw were coming together better than I expected.

With five days until my tattoo, I headed off to the island of

Koh Rong for some relaxation. Thinking about the trip, I realised again that only I am responsible for what happens - both good and bad. When travelling alone, you don't have to be alone. For me solitude is never good. So, as new people and experiences came into play, my comfort zone felt like it was being pushed and pulled out of shape. It sounds a small thing but how many people are really comfortable with talking to complete strangers? That is one of the fundamentals of experiences like this, you need to develop your self-confidence - and there had been no shortage of that so far.

At times during the trip I really began to think and feel that anything is possible and I had started to truly believe in my abilities once more. So, the tattoo would almost feel like a suit of armour, a badge of honour to wear with pride. After all, the words 'strength, love, pride, belief' had echoed around my head since Sri Lanka and the tattoo would now form the basis of that meaning. As the negativity of not working in my previous environment slowly drained away, so was my short fuse. My temper has been an issue at various points throughout my life. Now, slowly but surely, I was overcoming it. I was also realising just how much I missed family and friends but, at this moment, I had no desire to return to England to live. I dreamt for years about 'living the dream', and even though it had been hard at times, why would I wish to go back to the same existence as before? No way. The pull away from consumerism and materialistic living was becoming too great.

On Koh Rong I was more than happy in a bamboo bungalow with a family of geckos for company and playing with a five week old langur monkey in the bar. Abandoned by his mother in the jungle, there he'd been found by someone from the resort who had since been looking after him. What experiences I'd had, first dogs and cats on Ko Lanta, then playing with tigers in Chiang Mai, and now the playful, funny and tiniest little thing in Cambodia. The smallest things often give the most pleasure; feeding a cute little monkey by hand certainly fitted that bill.

Koh Rong, with its azure blue sea and pristine beaches, was

an excellent place to unwind – and unwind I did, topping off three great days of relaxation with a little 'horizontal jogging' with a lovely waitress from the resort.

Returning to Sihanoukville, I had now just over a day to wait before I was to get my first tattoo. More than a little trepidation started to set in, the usual questions running through my mind. What if I don't like it? What if it turns out really awful? And, most of all, how much will it bloody hurt? Only natural for a tattoo virgin, I guess. Taking Mark's advice, I visited the local pharmacist for some Tramadol, a strong post-operative pain-killer widely recommended by tattoo artists, due to its non blood thinning properties.

Checking my emails that evening, I saw that I had received one from Ecoteer about the Volunteer Leader Co-ordinator job I'd applied for back in early December. After scanning through to the juicy bits and reading between the lines, I'd come a close second in the interviews. A little disappointed, but it also said that they wanted to offer me another job that had recently become available. Bit of a quandary there. Only during the last week or so had I booked flights to New Zealand and, to be honest, there was no way I was going to miss out on visiting there a second time. So, with a heavy heart I sent a reply saying I couldn't take up their offer but I did ask if they could leave me on file.

Sometimes things happen like this, I'd waited for so long to hear whether or not I'd got the job, it got to the point where I had to make a decision about what to do next. In this case, maybe I'd missed out on an opportunity, but realistically, I couldn't have waited around any longer, I had to carry on. Maybe it just wasn't meant to be. Perhaps destiny had other plans for me, possibly something even better. Maybe that's what awaited me in New Zealand. I didn't know of course but in my current positive, upbeat mood, I did consider it a possibility.

The next morning, worrying about my forthcoming tattoo appointment, I pushed my lunch around the plate, not really hungry but knowing this would be my last chance to eat for the rest of the day. When I walked into the tattoo parlour just before two o'clock, Mark was busy with the stencil. By the time he had made all the necessary adjustments, it was nearly five o'clock before the first hum of the tattoo gun sounded.

'Right, here we go. I'll just do a couple of lines to see how we go' he said, guiding the tattoo machine towards my arm.

The sensation was like a cat scratching it's claw slowly across my arm.

'Jesus,' I thought. 'Is it going to be like this for the next five hours?'

No was the simple answer. It wasn't five hours - it was seven - and the pain was ten times worse. I'd taken two Tramadol tablets half an hour before I walked into the studio – and five more during the marathon session as the dull, scratching, grinding feeling grew steadily worse. As he started creating the lion's mane, blood poured from my arm. Never in my life had I endured so much discomfort for so long. I'd rather sit through an episode of 'Friends' with my head stuck in a blender than endure this again. On more than one occasion Mark became quite frustrated with me, saying things like: - 'Fuck me, that hurts there, don't it?' Yes, it bloody well did - a lot. I was reminded on more than one occasion that I was a willing volunteer. In other words - 'Put up and shut up, Phil.' With that thought engaging my weary head, I gritted my teeth, sat back in the chair and thought of every positive thing I could. Five Tramadol, several bottles of water, four cans of coke, four cups of tea and half a pack of cigarettes later, my first tattoo was finished. Having sat through what would probably be two or three tattoo sessions all at once, somewhere around the midnight hour, my arm felt and looked like a piece of raw meat.

Looking in the mirror during our many breaks, I'd seen the tattoo taking shape, taking pictures as it came together and each time it looked better and better. Now there it was in all its glory, my guardian lion, a beautiful mixture of golden colours, sitting proudly on my shoulder. Mark had done a fantastic job; a true professional, his attention to the smallest detail was amazing. I got a six out of ten for my bravery and whimpering too, which apparently was good for a first tattoo. I obviously don't have the same masochistic tendencies as those who say that pain is close to pleasure. The only pleasure for me was seeing his fantastic creation right at the very end. With more than seven hours of adrenaline firmly flowing through my body, my first impression was that it had certainly been worth the wait and the copious amounts of pain I had endured. In a doped up daze, I thanked a rather pissed off looking tattoo artist and left for a much needed beer before bed.

The following day I boarded a bus for the four hour journey to Koh Kong, a nondescript town used as a stopover for the Cambodia/Thai border crossing at Cham Yeam. I was to stay here for two nights, visiting the Cardamom Mountains, then travel to Bangkok for a further three nights before flying to Hanoi, have a wander around and then on to New Zealand. Sitting on the bus, thinking about the events of the previous twenty-four hours, I suddenly became quite conscious of the German lady sat next to me. She kept covering her mouth and nose with a scarf. Out of the corner of my eye I caught her glance in my direction more than once. At first I ignored it, then thought; 'Is it me who smells?' I started to develop a bit of a complex and tried to grab a sneaky sniff of my arm which, being wrapped in cling film and weeping large amounts of pus and ink onto the bandage holding it all together, didn't look particularly attractive. Nonetheless, this lady had a face like someone had shit in her handbag. I was quite annoyed about it and really wanted to say something, but didn't. Then, when the old bus broke down and we all got off, it gave me a chance to see whether my arm smelled or not. It didn't. It did look pretty bad but did she have to make such a song and dance about it? Probably not, but what do you do? Luckily when we got back on the bus she sat somewhere else but in her place I got another German, and she stank of body odour. Problem moved, problem solved and then reversed. Touché!

After two days of doing nothing much, other than washing

and looking after my arm, I boarded another bus for the ten hour journey across the border towards Bangkok. No surprise really, but there were yet more bribes and corruption on display as seventy or so people descended from several buses all at once, all melting in the midday sun and patiently waiting for the Cambodian authorities to start processing exit visas. First one, then another 'official' stepped out of the office, asking people whether they wished to pay $5 to get their exit stamp from inside the office. Ninety slow and frustrating minutes passed before we were able to resume our journey to Bangkok.

Bangkok for three nights would be enough for most people. I'd only ever flown there in transit and had heard so much about it that I thought it would be probably a good idea to have a look at this amazing city for myself. As a gap filler, they don't come more hectic or busier than downtown Bangkok. It's one of those cities that never sleeps and everywhere is a constant bustle of noise. But that is one of the endearing things about it. I checked out the impressive shopping malls and one or two go-go bars, which were actually very clean, safe and fun places to visit, though a little expensive. And no visit to Bangkok is complete without seeing an eye-opening ping-pong show, purely for research purposes of course – and time well spent.

There are amazing markets that sell anything and everything. Chatuchak is the largest market in Thailand and even sells all kinds of animals and dogs - which do not look right dressed up in little clothes. Searing humidity, large skyscrapers, constant hassle by taxi drivers, lady boys giggling and preening themselves on every corner, touting for unsuspecting men - yep, welcome to Bangkok. I had a great time though, doing and seeing what I needed to before taking my flight to Hanoi.

***

Hanoi is a really eclectic place, the city of a million motorbikes, a bustling, busy city - one you will either love or hate. With the constant, annoying noise of horns, it certainly makes you watch every step you take. I liked the fact that there was always something going on. On every street corner there would be someone cooking, or sat on a motorbike balancing a logic defying load, or pavement sellers trying to extract as many tourist dollars as they can. It is an experience that really shouldn't be missed, if given the chance. The people are friendly and will help at any opportunity but they'll also seize that moment to try and convince you that you really do need that poor quality T shirt, wallet or motorbike taxi ride.

After a couple of days though, the urge to leave Hanoi becomes overwhelming. A 380km overnight train journey to Sapa, a glorious market town high amongst the hills in the Lao Cai province of North Western Vietnam, near the Chinese border, staying for three days on a homestay with a local family and trekking through the villages and ranges there, seemed like a jolly good and interesting way to do it.

Hooking up with a cross section of people from different countries and backgrounds, I shared a great conversation with an Australian chap from the hostel in a not too dissimilar situation to mine. At 32 he had reached a crossroads in life. A nice guy with a lovely girlfriend, and yet he was still somehow unfulfilled. He was bored and fed up with his life, he had fallen into the familiar trap of taking a job that didn't inspire or push him. He was looking for that something, he told me. As vague as that might sound, I understood him fully.

How many of us are in that same position? Too many of us, yet so many still stick with their safety nets, always thinking, never doing, feeling lost, hopeless and discontent. There is always a way out, I told him, but we have to be brave enough to recognise that change is the answer we need. Along his journey through life, only he could decide what to do about it. There was one thing he decided to do that I definitely couldn't help him with. I politely turned down his invitation to join him in trying the local delicacy; too many thoughts of my own dog and Ko Lanta made it a mission impossible.

***

It had been just over a week since my permanent reminder of Cambodia, a week of waking up every morning with my bed sheets covered in dead scabs. By now though, my tattoo had almost fully healed. It made me feel proud every time I cast an admiring glance at it in any mirror I could find. This was still a novelty and it did feel strange to see this work of art on my arm, almost like a tribal badge, my very own guardian lion watching over me and guiding me forwards. With my fears over how it would turn out now gone and replaced with defiance and pride, I knew this had been an inspired move. In fact, when I was in Sri Lanka, I'd thought about having the words 'Strength, Love, Pride, Belief' etched onto my forearm but now I realised that this is exactly what my tattoo meant to me. Good job I'd had the sense to wait until I found exactly what I'd wanted.

When I arrived back in Hanoi, I had just two hours until another bus picked me up to take me to the UNESCO World Heritage Site at Ha Long Bay, a part of Vietnam recently featured in a 'Top Gear' special. There I was joining a 'Booze Cruise' on a traditional Junk boat with a rather enthusiastic group of young backpackers from our hostel. I noticed that most of the other people on the bus seemed to be under 22, but hey, this was my trip too and I wasn't going to let age become a barrier. That night, I felt like 'Frank the Tank' would make an appearance again at some point, probably once alcohol had been introduced into the proceedings. I was all set to join in the frivolity of stripping half naked, supping 'bum rum' forfeits out of peoples' bottoms, possibly having to snog boys or swap clothes with young women with barely any 'grass on the pitch' alongside the 'eager to get pissed as quickly as possible' group of rowdy 'twatpackers.' Fortunately, before 'Frank' could put in an appearance, I realised that no matter how hard I tried to 'look cool' and fit in, I couldn't - and I would have looked a complete fool trying. Realistically, how can a 41 year old man compete with folk half his age?

So using middle-aged, responsible thinking, I, and a couple of similar aged Aussies, watched from the safety zone of the bar as everyone else gradually became more and more inebriated, playing drinking games that looked fun - but I was so glad I hadn't taken part in. A good night nonetheless.

During the night, my new companion broke down in tears when, after explaining about my book, he confessed to being at a similar point where he just didn't know what he was doing with his life anymore. A good job, great girlfriend, house etc. just didn't seem enough. He, like the Australian guy in Sapa, had a piece missing but just wasn't sure what to do about it.

An hour of chatting later, I'd convinced him that the answers he wanted were inside him, he would just have to find them. Meeting people along the way provides the strength to keep going with your own journey but if I can help and inspire others to overcome their own daemons, then how great can that be? Thinking about the past five months, I'd not found my own answers yet, but knew they were getting closer. I felt drawn towards New Zealand, but would it provide the answers I was looking for?

***

On the journey back to Hanoi I started to think long and hard about another area of my life that, for the past five months or so on the road, I had not given a second thought to; my nicotine habit.

Its funny how, in our lives, we can find the resolve to overcome some of the highest hurdles and problems, ones that push us to the very limits, yet so many of us struggle desperately to slay the monster that is nicotine.

Thinking back to the day my wife announced that she was leaving, the first thing I did, after picking myself back up off the floor, was to go to the local shop and buy a bottle of vodka and a packet of rolling tobacco. Even though I had not smoked during the previous twelve months, I still reverted back to the old habit. I'd lost count how many times I'd tried or succeeded in stopping, yet time and time again I'd start again - and this last time was no different.

One thing that I'd always prided myself on over the years though, was my fitness level. I used to regularly run three miles with the dog, at least twice a week; I'd cycled to work, or just for pleasure and hiked whenever I could. By the time I'd started this trip though, I was back on the cigs again. In the beginning they had combatted the lonely and emotional times or became the friend in the bar when there was no one else to chat to. But as the trip progressed so too did my nicotine input. I had come to rely on them more and more. By this time, nearly twenty a day had become quite normal. Frightening for a 'social smoker' who usually only smoked two, maybe three, a day.

So I decided that, before I arrived in New Zealand I would again quit. Having read Allen Carr's book 'Easy Way to Stop Smoking' on at least two previous occasions, I knew what I had to do, but could I do it, could I defeat this little bastard again? The answer was simple; I could.

It was just a matter of realising that, instead of simply thinking about what I would like to do and doing nothing, I simply had to do it. I reminded myself again that the answers to most of our problems, fears, issues, whatever they might be in life, are usually already inside of us. We actually know the answers already but they are usually buried within our subconsciousness. We always make one excuse or another not to take action to address something we want to change in our lives. We know that we have to do something, but it's much easier to ignore it, hoping the problem will go away. But how often does it? This time, for health reasons more than anything, I knew I had to stop smoking again. Besides, being a Lancastrian, there was no bloody way I'd be paying $18NZ - around nine quid - for a packet of cigarettes.

This time there would be no going back. If I could overcome all the hurdles that I had since my marriage had ended, the blips I suffered at the beginning of the trip or the loneliness of travelling solo, then I could defeat the monster and slay him from my body and mind once and for all. I was a stronger person than I gave myself credit for and this was a great way to prove to myself how strong the power of the mind can really be, if we just let it happen.

So I made my decision. On Sunday night I went to a bar in Hanoi to watch some FA Cup football and there I finished my beer, smoked the last cigarette in my packet and became a non smoker once again. By now my health had begun suffering again and only the next day as I gasped and wheezed, running to check in at Hanoi Airport, I realised that my decision had been the right one. This once very fit and able man was not as fit as he used to be. I needed to sort it out and fast.

10
The Adventures of the Red Shed

The flight from Hanoi to Ho Chi Minh City was largely uneventful. Mind you, saying that, I was expecting it to be. The same applied from there to Kuala Lumpur for my transit to Christchurch. Too good to be true? Yep, that proved to be exactly the case. Upon landing in Kuala Lumpur and progressing through immigration, I wasn't allowed to board the next plane as I had overseen the small matter of booking an exit flight from New Zealand. My heart sank and my knees wobbled as the young Malaysian man informed me that I would not be going anywhere unless I provided evidence of an onward ticket from New Zealand - and I hadn't even decided where the hell to go next. Worrying that I would miss out on visiting New Zealand for the second time, I spent three frustrating hours trying to book an exit flight, having decided on Melbourne, Australia as my next port of call. Finally, after being handed my boarding confirmation, I settled into my seat, exhausted and shaking, only thirty minutes ahead of the scheduled departure time. I then remembered that I'd not had a cigarette for over twenty-four hours, so I had my in flight meal, took two valium and lost the next nine hours. I finally arrived at Christchurch on a Tuesday afternoon to be greeted in true English style; it was raining, hard. After five months in Asia in temperatures around 31 degrees, I come here and it's bloody raining. When Captain Cook colonised the place he must have brought the British weather over with him.

I was staying in Christchurch for a week with Julia, a lovely German girl who volunteered with me at Lanta Animal Welfare centre. The suburb of Richmond was to be my base for the next week before going to the first of my 'Workaway' volunteer projects in Oamaru. Julia, and her partner Justin, gave me the full use of their 50cc moped so I was able to zip around the city, sightseeing in much the same way as I had in Ko Lanta. It was nice to rewind in my mind back to that very happy month spent looking after the cats and dogs.

***

The day after I'd arrived was an important date here in Christchurch. On February 22nd 2011 an earthquake decimated virtually all of the city centre, claiming 185 lives, with countless others wounded and homeless. A year later, as I rode around the city, many streets were still closed, there were shored up buildings on every corner and gaping holes in the roads. Since 2010, there have been over 7600 mini earthquakes and tremors recorded throughout the country, but on that February afternoon at 12.51pm, the epicentre was only 5km away from Christchurch and it ripped right through the very heart of this once beautiful city, destroying it in an instant.

Watching a TV programme that evening about the earthquake, it was wonderful to see how the whole community had since pulled together. There is a real phoenix rising attitude here, and everyone feels it. It felt good to experience just how that strength of spirit could warm people's souls.

Years ago, I remember speaking with German friends as they described their country's conditions after the Second World War. That same spirit appears to be here now - a proud, defiant, undefeated attitude, a determination to pull together as a city and rebuild, not only their own lives, but also those of their neighbours and that of the community. Maybe we can only imagine how it must feel to be caught up in something as terrifying and life changing as an earthquake when we become involved. The impact it has had on individuals has been life changing in so many ways. Throughout the decimated streets porta-cabin communities have sprung up and I even spotted a fridge being used as a book exchange. Clearly the Kiwi's don't lose their sense of humour, even in challenging times like these.

***

My first impression of New Zealanders was that they all seem to want to enjoy their lives as much, and as often, as they can. Everywhere is geared up for outdoor living with people running, cycling or walking in the parks, creating their own work/life balance.

Speaking of a healthy lifestyle, four days had passed since I'd last had a cigarette. No doubt the fact that hardly anyone here seemed to smoke had helped. The best thing to do when you stop smoking is to surround yourself with non-smoking people. Maybe that is why quitting this time seemed easier than on previous occasions. That was surprising – yet encouraging. I'd bought some cheap running trainers too and was working out again. I was really enjoying my time in Christchurch and looking forward to exploring this beautiful country. After over five months sweating profusely in Asia, I felt so happy to be returning to a first world country.

A first world country it most definitely is, but it suddenly occurred to me one day as I was 'downloading my hard drive,' so to speak; just where the bloody hell was the bum gun?

'What's a bum gun?' a friend I was chatting to on Skype once asked me.

'You know, the hosepipe with the trigger on the end, next to the toilet."

'The what?'

'You mean you've never heard of it?' I replied, quite shocked, assuming that everyone either had or used one.

Without trying to be crude, I got up off the toilet, and looked frantically around for the friend I'd become so used to in Asia.

Where was he? Then it suddenly dawned on me that bum guns are unique to Asia. So, I would have to use toilet paper again. It was a shock I can tell you. How can this be right? I'd spent so much time in primitive environments and mostly all had a bum gun or a bucket of water, either doing the job perfectly well. Then I come to a first world country and guess what? No bloody bum gun. This was strange at first. Travelling in places where the hygiene standards were dubious, to say the least, and then coming here, having to waste paper and time on something that a squirt of the gun can quickly sort out. I have to admit, I was so used to my daily mini colonic, it had become second nature. God, I'll miss my hose.

***

After a great week in Christchurch, the time came to move on. Oamaru would be my first stop. I'd arranged to volunteer at 'Chillawhile Backpackers,' as part of the 'Workaway' volunteer scheme. 'A hidden gem', the advert read, 'providing a backdrop for musos, artists etc. to hook up and help. Exchange two and a half hours per day for board, enjoy great experiences and meet lots of people from around the globe.' It could be good, I thought.

I suppose now that we're at this stage I'd better explain what 'Workaway' is. Quite simply, it's a volunteer scheme that allows people to work for a given period of time in either their own or another country, learning different skills whilst integrating into local cultures and meeting new people along the way. All you need to do is register, create a personal profile and start looking for any project that you fancy doing in your country of choice. Simple! Choose things like working in hotels or backpacker hostels, working with animals or teaching English, to name but a few.

After one or two enquiries here and there, I'd applied to volunteer at Chillawhile Backpackers lodge. In exchange for free accommodation at the hostel I would be making beds, hoovering up, gardening and undertaking general handyman duties. As the hostel had a painting room, three guitars and enough drums to open a shop, there would be no shortage of entertainment from anyone that fancied having a go, including myself after a few beers no doubt!

Oamaru, a popular destination with tourists and travellers alike, is the largest town in North Otago and lies in-between Christchurch and Dunedin, and famous for its little blue penguins and its historic quarter in the heart of the town. I travelled on an Atomic Shuttle bus and arrived there early on a Tuesday afternoon. My first impression of the town made me think that this could be a nice place to volunteer, quaint, quiet, yet enough to keep me busy and use as a base for exploring nearby attractions on my time off. At the hostel I met some of the other travellers and volunteers, a mixture of ages from a variety of backgrounds, including John, a likeable Canadian chap of a similar age to myself - but also very loud and unfortunately without a volume control fitted.

John was an avid bike rider and the proud owner of a large Kawasaki 650 motorbike which he'd purchased when he first arrived in New Zealand. Despite having previously only ridden on the back of a 'Raleigh Chopper' or on mopeds, I pleaded with him for two days to be allowed to ride pillion on a trip to visit the Moeraki Boulders, a natural rock formation on the beach.

One afternoon, after we'd finished working the day's shift, John gave in to my pleas. I was excited by the prospect of riding pillion - but a little apprehensive all the same. For the 100km journey I had to put my faith and trust in a man in charge of his new toy - an obvious penis extension. My fears that I'd be shitting bricks were soon realised. What an amazing adrenaline rush though, seeing a new country from such a different angle. Fearing for my life as he wound the throttle up to more than 100kmph, all my internal organs seemed to rise in the direction of my mouth, leaving me clinging on for dear life, shutting my eyes and saying a silent prayer to the Great Man upstairs, asking for us to arrive at our destination in one piece. We weaved along, up and down beautifully straight but hilly roads, cutting a path between mountain ranges on one side and the ocean on the other. It was a stunning day and the blueness of the sky and the rich green of the countryside combined spectacularly to make me appreciate the breathtaking beauty of New Zealand.

Thankfully, my prayer was answered and I arrived, pale faced and sweating. Getting off the bike wasn't easy though; I had been gripping the bar at the back so tightly that both hands ached and stung with pins and needles. Still, what an amazing experience, one that had given me something else to think about; how would I actually see more of this amazing country when I left Oamaru?

Ever since I'd arrived it had crossed my mind more than once that I didn't have my own wheels. It was so easy to get about in Asia - by bus, train or even the ubiquitous tuk-tuks. Here though was different. I could get to most towns and cities, no problem. I could travel by shuttle buses, The Kiwi Experience, Naked Bus or Atomic Shuttles. But, to get anywhere from there would be difficult, expensive or both. It was bugging me that I could miss out on so much of what New Zealand had to offer. The thought of spending two months or so bumming lifts around this beautiful country had me squirming nervously every time I thought about it. I considered hiring a car but, at around $45NZ a day, it worked out far too expensive. There was, I realised, only one thing for it; to actually see this amazing country the way I really wanted to, I would have to buy a car. There was no other realistic way. I needed the independence and the freedom to just take off as and when I wanted to.

The following day, as I walked across the harbour, I did my sums and decided that it would make perfect sense to buy a car, then sell it before my time here came to an end, in nine weeks time. Setting a budget of 1500 dollars, I began scouring the small ads on 'Trade Me,' Kiwi's version of E-bay. I soon found the sort of car I was looking for - a Toyota Corolla, sporting red and 23 years old, recently serviced and bang on budget. I called up and arranged to view it that day. I liked the guy selling it and after a short test drive about town, I agreed to buy it. Then, as we were about to start exchanging documents and cash, I noticed its registration. PL1540. Nothing odd about that you may think, but you would be wrong as PL are the initials of my name - Philip Lee. A coincidence? Or something more, a sign, maybe? It certainly seemed so to me. As they say; 'It had my name written all over it,' I was obviously meant to have it; a good omen, so to speak. So, trusting my instincts, I handed over the cash. Finally I had my own wheels. Get in! Thirty minutes later I was cruising the harbour area of Oamaru looking for little blue penguins, feeling pleased as punch with my new 'pimp my ride' purchase.

The following day I set off with Maria, a French volunteer, on a road trip to Mount Cook and beyond, the car loaded up with a sleeping bag and nearly new tent I'd found and repaired. I fully intended to make use of these from now on, camping wherever possible, saving money on hostel fees. Two breath-taking days later, the sheer wonder of Mount Cook and other sights had been seen from this new angle. There was a clunk every time the gear shifted from second to third or back, but sod that, I was back on the road and enjoying the freedom of it. The scenery kept getting better and better and we arrived back in Oamaru fully invigorated and ready to start work again. Later, intending to head off into town, I turned the ignition key – and nothing happened. Bugger.

I called the local sparky and $132.32NZ later, a new alternator solved the problem. Was this the inspired purchase I thought it had been? Well, not if I end up spending any more bloody money on it, it won't. At least the new air freshener smelled nice and the car now had its nickname - 'The Red Shed.' With over 396,000 genuine kilometres on the clock, I was a little concerned that the engine might blow up, but sod it, if it did, I'd worry about it then.

A day later and my week or so of volunteering in Oamaru was over. I'd had a great time, met lots of nice people, played guitar every night, earned my keep and still managed to see the first part of my Southern Island trip. Now I needed to set off down the coast to meet and engage with more local people, but how could I get more involved in meeting them? Chatting to those in shops and garages was great but, as I'd be spending most of my time with other travellers, I thought how nice it would be to get to know the locals better.

There was only one thing for it, if I wanted to get more involved with local people and learn about the Kiwi way of life, I would have to go 'Couch Surfing.' Before you say it, couch surfing is not standing on a settee pretending it is a surfboard; it's a great concept that connects travellers with local people who are willing to allow them into their homes free of charge. Confused? Yes, so was I when the idea was first mentioned to me. How could that idea possibly work? Actually it works very well. The idea behind couch surfing is that you register to be a host or a surfer. The host will put certain criteria on his/her page and the surfer does the same. When the surfer requests a couch for the night, the host can decide by checking out their profile whether it will be theirs they will be sleeping on. Simple.

After putting my profile together and deciding to 'surf' in Dunedin, I tested the water, looking for a suitable host. Having been given a reference earlier in the week by John, the Canadian guy whose Kawasaki bike had nearly destroyed my sphincter muscle, I was accepted by Rog. After the drive down, some ten minutes after knocking repeatedly on his front door, a fifty something year old punk rocker made his way quite merrily up the hill towards me, grinning and waving.

"G'day Phil, nice to meet you," he said, puffing and panting so much it was like listening to an obscene phone call.

"Ey up Rog" I replied, shaking hands with the enthusiastic, half pissed and happy bovver boy.

That was the start of four days of the highly enjoyable and beneficial scheme known as couch surfing.

"He's an awesome dude," John had said. "You'll be cool with Rog, he's an old punk but what a nice guy."

How right he was. Sitting in his front room, totally new to this concept of inviting yourself into a stranger's house and crashing on their sofa, it seemed surreal but, by reintroducing the basic core values of a civilised society - honesty and trust - then it should always work, provided both parties keep to their side of the bargain.

"So Rog," I said a little apprehensively, "how do you want me to do this?'

"Oh, it'll be alright, it'll work itself out, just make a meal one night."

'Hmm, well okay,' I thought, 'let's just run with this. Two strangers thrust together could be a lot of fun.' And that is exactly what it turned out to be. That night we went to the local Muso's club in Dunedin where he told me about himself. A photographer in his spare time, Rog had been privileged to have photographed some of the world's top rock and punk acts, including one of my all time favourite bands, Iron Maiden. Fascinating, Rog was a real character and just the sort of person I enjoyed meeting. So how did I repay his kindness as a host who had to put up with me? Well, the first thing I did was wash up. His last surfer was a French chap who didn't do anything during his stay so, to hopefully get my feedback score off to a flying start, I washed up some manky plates, cleaned his bathroom, which quite frankly was disgusting, and fixed the broken toilet seat.

How this scheme works successfully is down to the surfer and host dynamics but, as the surfer, you should, or rather must, do something to help out your host. Cooking a meal is a favourite or wash/tidy up, or take a pet for a walk - it all helps and gives the feeling that you have not just bummed your way onto someone's couch for a free ride. I tried to do a bit of everything and it worked really well.

On the Monday morning, after days filled with good laughs fuelled by plenty of alcohol, I thanked him for letting me sleep on a mattress in his front room, said goodbye and headed for the hour and a half's drive to Middlemarch. I'd had a lot of fun couch surfing and would recommend it to anyone who wants to try something completely different. I would definitely be doing it again. But would every future experience be as good as this one I wondered?

***

Starting in the town of Middlemarch, the Otago Rail Trail is an old goldmine railway line that stretches as far as the township of Clyde some 150kms away. The trail affords some truly breathtaking scenery through Central Otago, an absolute pleasure to cycle in the beautiful, early autumn weather, taking in the great contours of the land and admiring a wide variety of birds and animals.

A wonderful day's cycling ended after 60km in the quaint, if not rather forgotten, town of Ranfurly. Here it seemed that the average family tree didn't have many branches attached to it. The darts being thrown in the local bar seemed to somehow freeze in mid air when I walked in later that evening. Still never mind, the beer was welcome, even if I wasn't.

I hadn't realised that Central Otago is actually the coldest place in New Zealand. That night I almost froze to death in my tent as the temperature plummeted to zero degrees. I'd failed to nab a ground mat of any sorts, so the night was spent wrapped head to foot in as many layers as I had with me. And it still wasn't enough. I shivered all night, the cold chilling right through to my bones. Unsurprisingly, I had a crap night's sleep. Still, it's all fun and part of the great experience of travel - isn't it?

The second day started much the same as the first, beautiful and warm, although early into the day's riding my knee had started playing up, so I needed to stop en-route to buy a rather expensive anti-inflammatory. Thankfully, it became easier after that.

Towards the end of another glorious day, around 8km from the camp-site where I'd be staying the night, I stopped for a coffee and slice of cake. As I was on the way out of the café, I acknowledged another cyclist on the way in. We ended up sharing a really interesting conversation. Paul, a man looking very well for a man in his early fifties, was riding around the 1000km Southern Scenic Route on his mountain bike, raising money for two cancer charities in New Zealand - The Cancer Society and Cure Kids. I loved the cute little trailer attached to his bike, crammed full of gadgets, tent, ground sheet, in fact everything you could think of.

He told me more about why he was on this mission over some arduous, hilly and very difficult road trails - and in some diverse weather as well. His mother had passed away from cancer in the previous November and he'd since decided to honour her memory by doing this sponsored cycle ride. How people can find the resolve to help others, even in their own hour of need, never fails to amaze or inspire me. Paul, although obviously still upset over his mother's death, was proud of what he was achieving. His story made me even more determined to raise money for Bury Hospice by completing the Camino de Santiago later in the year.

Together we cycled those last 8 kms to the camp site and, when putting our tents up, he told me that even though today had been a scorcher, tonight would be just as cold as the previous night, if not colder. Acquiring a ground sheet from the plump, jolly park owner, I set my crib up for the night before going to the village pub. Over a few hard earned pints of Speights Old Dark, I told Paul of what I'd done so far on my travels and my planned walk for later in the year. We spoke of how helping others can enrich your own life. We agreed that giving a little something to others can be life-changing in so many different ways and how only those who had been in similar positions could ever really know how that felt. Paul is undoubtedly proud of his hard earned efforts in raising money for his chosen charities. He had only a few days to go before he finished his mammoth ride, having cycled it all in his own time - and all with a fused neck too. Like he said, his pain is a small price to pay for the reward his selfless act had brought to him - and for his mother's memory too.

Starting the next morning with a thicker head than normal, I slowly set off on the last 37km of the 150 km route. As my knee had all but given up, I limped into to the small town of Clyde around lunchtime. Tired yet happy, the shuttle bus then brought me back to Middlemarch.

Re-united with the Red Shed, I set off on the journey south, following the coastline to the next area of South Island on my itinerary - The Catlins. I was looking forward to an overnight stay in a hostel in Owaka. After spending the last two nights impersonating an ice lolly in my tent and the previous four on a mattress on the floor in Roger's living room, I was so glad to see a bed again. It even had an electric blanket. Get in! Hang on, it doesn't work. Still never mind, there were two thick duvets on the bed, and with the wind howling like a banshee outside, it had been an inspired move to choose not to camp again for the time being.

The following morning, having picked up a rather nice Dutch girl who would be my travel companion for the day, I made my way to the I-Site - or tourist information. With there being no mobile phone signals, their landline allowed the lady there to call McCleans Falls Holiday Park on my behalf. I'd contacted them some two months or so earlier regarding some voluntary carpentry work. As I hadn't received any replies, I'd kind of thought there was no point calling them but, as I was quite literally passing, it seemed daft not to. That proved to be the correct thought as, later that day, I met Paul Brydon the holiday park's owner. Even though there was no longer any joinery work needing to be done, Paul offered me a week's worth of gardening and painting in exchange for free food and accommodation - which turned out to be a garden shed. Well, it's what we'd call it back in the UK but, here on the park, it was one of a series of 'cabins' lining one side of the grounds. Parking up outside, I rather excitedly opened the shed door and was surprised by the interior. Rather like Doctor Who's Tardis, it was deceptively spacious. (Maybe I should be selling cupboards disguised as 'apartments' in London?) It had two single beds, a desk, kettle and heater. Well, bugger me, that's exactly what I needed, somewhere to write and chill out. The beds even had electric blankets - and they worked too.

After a lovely, warm night's sleep, I reported for work at 10 am on a lovely South Island day. I was given my petrol lawnmower and strimmer with instructions to 'make the place look great, Phil.' For the next seven days that's exactly what I did; I sweated and worked for five hours every day. Quite frankly when someone offers free food and accommodation, I will always do my best to give a good day's work in return. Kindness works two ways. It was hard work but so satisfying to see the forest transformed into lawns again. Even more satisfying was knowing that, by receiving great accommodation and food in exchange for just a few hours of my time, I was not only saving myself a small fortune, I also had plenty of free time to explore the Catlins area where the Cathedral Caves provided an amazing backdrop for seal spotting whilst walking for miles on stunning, unspoilt, isolated beaches. The Catlins is very remote and any down time meant a car journey to get anywhere, so my decision to buy the Red Shed was paying dividends. With the cliffs on one side and the quite magnificent views of the coast on the other, on a clear day this really was as close as it gets to paradise.

Paul was a lovely guy and left me to get on with the work, although one day, having reduced his lawns and borders to about as much stubble as I have on my head, I happened to be fixing the strimmer when he walked past. Exchanging conversation, it transpired that he was an ex-copper amongst other things. Telling him that I was a Senior Officer in the Prison Service and before that a carpenter, he suddenly said, "Well, listen, keep in touch when you go, we're always looking for good people here, you know. I can always sponsor you to come and work here."

It was strange how, by putting myself out a bit, working hard and honestly, this opportunity had come along - precisely what I was trying to achieve from the outset. And, like others before, it came out of the blue when I'd least expected it to.

The timing of this one couldn't have been better. Only a few days previously I'd found out quite by chance that the Civil Service were bringing out a voluntary redundancy package in the Prison Service - and I was eligible to apply. Some serious thought was needed though. Even though this was what I'd wanted, the package had to be right and something else needed to be put into its place. Could Paul's offer be that something?

It wasn't my only option either. When I first landed in New Zealand, I'd followed up a lead to join the New Zealand Correctional Services. To be honest though, the more thought I gave to that one, the less I could actually be bothered. As I was so fed up and disheartened with the job back in the UK, why would I want to put myself through all the same hassles in a different country? It's a fair point; if we are truly unhappy with something, then we should deal with and solve the problem, not just move it. Maybe I should listen to my own advice more and look outside the box? All of this proved that there were countless opportunities and possibilities out there, if I could only see them as that. At this stage it didn't matter - but it gave me more options to consider.

The problem was, I also seemed to be faced with several options on what to do next back home. I had to decide whether to extend the tenancy on my house or return to the UK and sell. My head now seemed to be swimming with new decisions to make. Even though it may seem nice, it wasn't. If I take voluntary redundancy, I would have a wad of cash in my pocket but no job. Hang on though; hadn't I wanted to be rid of that millstone from around my neck? Maybe I can't have my cake and eat it, but there were still some decisions that needed very careful thought.

Walking along the rather lovely Tautuku beach, close to the Cathedral Caves, I had the time and space to gaze and think of the options pressing at the minute. I had at this time reached a plateau on my trip and was having great difficulty in looking forward to the next part. I suppose everything had got on top of me, perfectly understandable when away from home and familiar surroundings for such a long period of time. Don't get me wrong, this is what I'd wanted but loneliness, having to sort things out and make decisions single-handedly did get the better of me at times. On top of that I hadn't seen any light at the end of any tunnel yet and I was also now really craving a nice female for company. So, the occasional dark cloud was always bound to appear overhead. It was simply a case of how long it would take to move - or not. Clearing my head as I walked back to the car, I remembered that afternoon I'd looked online and sent off emails aimed at places to volunteer in Australia and my mood lifted slightly as I thought of new possibilities and opportunities that may arise from it. Suddenly, I started to feel better.

Three hours later, the latest twist and turn unfolded. Recently I had been reflecting on missed opportunities, especially on what could have been with regards to the Volunteer Co-ordinators job in Malaysia. Checking my emails, there was one from Ecoteer asking for expressions of interest in this role again. How and why this has come about now, I'll never know but maybe this opening had come back for a reason. I'd spent an hour or so applying for new opportunities in Australia and Indonesia along with testing the water with an English teachers job in Taiwan - and now I had this to juggle too. So what do you do when this happens? Laugh or cry? I did neither. I decided to send a reply and then sit back and wait for things to come back to me.

***

It would have been so easy to carry on wearing the comfy slippers of the holiday park's great facilities but, after a great week here, I knew the time was right to leave my garden shed behind and head off again.

Driving towards Stewart Island, I spent most of the journey stopping off at various interesting places along the way. Eventually though, I parked the Red Shed at the harbour town of Bluff where I would board the ferry for the one hour crossing. I was rather looking forward to exploring this eco-island and doing some great walking.

Over the next two days I did just that, hooking up with a couple of great English people from my hostel. Walking along the path on a grey, overcast and rain filled day, it didn't surprise me when they told me that they were in a similar situation to myself, looking for something different. Both had felt a call to arms, so to speak, and were travelling to allow themselves the time and space they hoped would clear their minds and give clarity to their direction forwards.

Being in a good backpackers' hostel helped me too; there was a good mixed crowd over the weekend, and many a cheeky glass of wine was quaffed. I even had time to take part in the local pub's weekly Sunday night quiz, choosing the politically incorrect but nonetheless amusing team name of 'A Kiwi, a Bulldog and a Frog' made up from, yep you guessed it, New Zealand, England & France. Our team of three made a respectable 5th place, bringing a hearty cheer from the rest of the pub who'd had six members in their teams.

Soon enough though, time was called, time for me to move on again, back to the mainland and up to Te Anau to walk the Kepler Track, another of the Great Walks of New Zealand. Walking for three days certainly gave me time to be alone with my thoughts and the question of what I wanted to do when I returned to the UK returned into my mind.

The weather turned foul halfway through the first day. Being soaked to the bone on any walk is less than pleasant, but here in the Fjordlands when the rain appears it doesn't half fall and my gore-tex jacket had overlooked the small matter of the need to stay dry. One of the first things I would need to do when I returned would be to buy a new waterproof. They are far too expensive here.

Staying at Department Of Conservation huts is an absolute necessity if you want to walk this, or any of the other ten Great Walks of New Zealand, each offering a diverse and amazing experience of the sheer range and beauty of this amazing country's walking opportunities. The DOC huts en-route provide everything you need - a mattress, a roof over your head, a toilet and shower - but you must carry all your food, sleeping bag and even the pans you need to cook with. Pack light, but remember there are no shops here.

On the first night I settled into the bunkhouse and decided to start reading a book I'd picked up the previous day. Being a keen cyclist I'd been drawn to 'It's Not About the Bike,' Lance Armstrong's book about his battle with cancer. As I'm on my own journey, I felt it would be good for me to read it. How right I was. When I read about his battle with cancer I couldn't help but feel inspired. Cancer does not care whether or not its victim has money, nor does it care about the size of their house or car. That certainly makes you think about how we lead and conduct our everyday lives. Take me for example; here I was, complaining that I was lonely, or cold, or hungry - and here was a man who, given a less than a 3% chance of survival, became so determined to fight cancer and win. Reading his story was quite humbling and placed my own worries into perspective. Not only did it prove to be motivational and truly inspiring, it also helped me to regain my determination and focus.

After completing this wonderful hike through gorgeous forests and ridges, I awoke on the final day to a view from Heaven itself, descending through one of the most stunning cloud banks from the bunkhouse to Te Anau below.

I returned to my camp site a weary walker. On checking my emails I found out that my career break was to be extended further. I also received confirmation of a voluntary place in June, teaching English in Bali, Indonesia. So, after the month in Australia, I'd have somewhere to volunteer back in Asia. That was certainly something to look forward to, focussing again on teaching and helping young people in a far worse situation than my own. As an added bonus, I'd more than likely be reunited with my old friend, the bum-gun.

That night in Te Anau, with my mind now cleared, I devoured a rather large burger and bottle of red wine, making up for not eating enough fodder during the trek. The following day I headed for an overnight cruise to the nearby Doubtful Sound for an unforgettable trip through the Fjordlands, a stunning way to see this unforgettable part of the South Island.

Back in the eighteenth century whilst having a wander around Australia and New Zealand, Captain James Cook had proclaimed:- 'It's doubtful we can get down there.' The name stuck and nearly 300 years later, it was doubtful I would ever experience a cruise as amazing as this again. With the sheer variety of wildlife, rock formations and outstanding natural beauty, not to mention the bloody lovely buffets on board, it was well worth the money. Meeting fellow Brits, Margaret and Tricia, we shared tales of travelling. Both it seemed had reached crossroads in their lives too. They were travelling, looking for the answers to their situations. Whether they would find them, it was unclear but experiencing the wonders of travel would perhaps help, giving them the breathing space they needed to find a new focus. Great company those girls; we enjoyed a cracking 24 hours together before we parted company, heading our separate ways, all looking for what we should do with our lives.

From Doubtful Sound I headed for Milford Sound to walk part of the 32km Routeburn track, setting up camp at the quirky, if not slightly 'Deliverance' style, 'Gunns Camp,' some 8kms from the start of the track. The sand flies I'd been warned about appeared from nowhere and swarmed around my head as I pitched my tent. Being bitten to fuck by them is never pleasant and, in this part of South Island, the little shits were everywhere. It was so bad that, heading back to the tent after supper, I unzipped the door only to find a whole bunch of them hanging off the ceiling, lying in wait to ambush me. After launching several strong 'fuck off you bastards' in their direction as they relentlessly dive bombed me, I had no choice but to abandon ship in favour of a bunk in the nearby empty dormitory. Thank God for that empty dorm, it saved my sanity for two nights. Sand flies really know how to ruin a man's adventure.

Leaving the somewhat strange, but highly pleasant, local hosts of the camp, I was now heading towards Queenstown. Whilst in New Zealand, I had planned to throw myself out of a plane at some stage - preferably attached to a parachute. With this being the adventure capital of the world, it would have been a good place to do it but, for some money saving reason, I decided not to. I spent two days chilling instead. On one of those days I ate an enormous 'Ferg Burger' which literally have to be seen to be believed, and had to mountain bike the '7mile circuit' like a Trojan to work the bloody thing off. I also managed to meet up with the intrepid biker, Paul. Exchanging a warm greeting in the pub, it was good to catch up with him again. His mammoth cycle challenge now over, he'd raised well over $1000NZ towards his chosen charities. A fantastic sense of pride exploded from his chest as he described how proud his mother would have been of him. Not just her Paul, I was proud to have met you brother; your spirit shone through like a diamond in a pile of muck.

The next day I passed through Wanaka, heading for the Franz Joseph Glacier, somewhere I didn't want to miss. Driving into Franz Joseph village, the sheer beauty of its location was enough to hold my breath in suspense; to then go off and do a glacier walk the next day was incredible. Walking up to 2700 ft or 830m on a gloriously warm and cloud free day ensured the very best possible views of the glacier and valleys. It was quite simply, magnificent. I even refilled my water bottle from the glacier streams, so pure was the water.

By now I'd completely fallen in love with this island. 'The Lord of the Rings' movies were filmed here. I'd never really been a fan, so I didn't go on any 'anorak' trips to see where they were filmed; focusing instead on the other outstanding beauties New Zealand had to offer. I was really beginning to relish every moment I spent in this environment. What would be next I wondered?

Whilst in Franz Joseph I decided this time I would be skydiving. For the past eight days every morning had been bright and sunny. Would you believe it, on the day I'd booked to skydive there was a thick layer of cloud which never lifted. After four attempts throughout the morning to re-schedule, the day's jumps had to be cancelled. Relieved or pissed off, I wasn't sure but somehow it had to be done. How often would I get the chance to face my fears of skydiving? Shame, but I could still do this in the North Island, probably at Lake Taupo.

Leaving Franz Joseph behind for a drive northwards up the East coast, I stopped overnight in Greymouth. It turned out to be a case of grey by name, grey by nature. There was very little of interest but it did break up the seven hour journey to the Abel Tasman National Park. Named after the first European explorer to sight New Zealand, this walk had been repeatedly recommended by many travellers, so I wanted to fit it in before leaving South Island. I wasn't left disappointed either; the walking here was simply beautiful. A great first day's tramp along the coastal track walk on another stunning autumn day ended when I arrived at the floating 'Aquapackers' hostel moored up in Anchorage Bay. What a great way to spend a night, holed up with ten other people on a boat with a bottle of red wine. I soon found myself jumping off the top deck into the quite cold but nicely refreshing sea with a couple of nice German and Spanish girls. I'd started the day in a really foul mood, so I set myself that goal when I landed at the boat. No matter how bloody cold it might be, I would be throwing myself off. I hate being in a bad mood, especially when I'm not sure exactly why.

The following morning I left the boat and arrived back at my campsite feeling rejuvenated. After a couple of further days without any socially challenging conversations, I felt ready to head into the North Island. Only one thing left to do though before I left. Taking advantage of a thoroughly miserable day, I booked the old faithful 'Red Shed' into the local garage for its half yearly WOF - Warranty of Fitness - the Kiwi equivalent to the British MOT test. Considering 'The Red Shed' is over 21 years old and has some 400,000km on the clock, this old boy doesn't half drive well. Even so, would he let me down now after all we've been through? I hoped not. I had to sell it in three weeks time; the last thing I needed was to spend a lot of money on it just to make it saleable.

I was extremely relieved to find out that all the car needed was two rear tyres. Bridging time while the garage fitted two pre worn tyres - at a cost of $130NZ - I visited the town of Motueka. For whatever reason, I started to feel down and low once more. After aimlessly wandering around the nondescript shops, I crossed the road, making my way back to the garage when I found myself drawn to a crystal and healing shop. Deciding I needed something to help align my spiritual balance again, I wandered in and, looking around, I was drawn towards an amethyst stone.

"Hello, nice to meet you," said Gail, the rather nice owner of the shop. After engaging in conversation with her, telling her about my travels and of helping others along the way, she looked at me with sympathetic eyes, mouth down-turned, as I told her how I was starting to become lonely and fed up, but wasn't sure why.

"I want to help you," she said.

Moving over to a display stand in the centre of the shop she looked up and down before finally picking an Amethyst pendant and handing it to me.

"There you are, try that."

"It's lovely, but I can't afford it," I replied, "I'll stick with the stone I've picked, thanks."

She looked at me again, "No, I want to give it to you."

I was so taken aback; it was worth $24, yet she wanted to give it to me. She asked me for a big hug. I was so overwhelmed by this stranger's humanity, I almost cried there and then. She wrote my details and the forthcoming book's title down and wished me every bit of love and luck for the remainder of my journey. I left the shop almost floating, finding some new strength from this random act of kindness. The love and kindness shown by Gail not only restored my faith and belief in myself but also in humanity as a whole.

The next day, I jumped into the Red Shed and made my way northwards towards Nelson to spend a night there before jumping on the ferry for the three hour crossing to Wellington in the North Island. Visiting a bookshop on the main street before checking in, I was pleased to find the Lance Armstrong sequel and also a book by William Pike, a young Kiwi chap who lost his leg after being crushed during a volcanic eruption of Mount Ruapehu in 2007. Again, I felt drawn towards another story that would undoubtedly inspire and motivate me.

After spending a crap night in a downtown Wellington backpackers, I started the next day in a dreadfully foul mood, unable yet again to shake it. Nothing would move it until I picked those books up. Only by thumbing through them did I stop feeling sorry for myself and try to refocus again. I know what the problem is. Travelling on your own can play havoc with your mind at times, especially if you can't find the kind of inspirational, motivational company or conversation to share with someone. This is why I'd had so many blips of late. Looking back at where I'd been, at what I'd done, I was struggling to put where I was going into perspective. I had to try and stop 'solving' everything and enjoy this wonderful, lucky to be able to live it experience. It was difficult, but reading about Lance Armstrong's cancer battle or William Pike's harrowing story gave me inspiration. They had both found the strength to carry on; quite simply I had to do so too. No one said this trip would be easy. At times maybe I hadn't given myself enough credit for what I was doing. Luckily, after sleeping with my crystal under the pillow the following night, I awoke feeling a lot more positive.

Leaving Wellington, I spent the next six hours strapped to the driving seat of the Red Shed on my way to walk the Tongariro Crossing, arguably the best one day hike in New Zealand, if not the world. The Tongariro Alpine Crossing is an amazing 19km walk. On a clear day it is simply stunning and today was such a day. After my blip on Friday 13th, I was determined to rediscover my 'mojo.' Halfway into the crossing I had a chance to take a side trip and climb Mount Ngauruhoe. Standing at 2287metres it gives an interesting offshoot climb to the crossing. With a pitch of around 65 degrees and no firm path aside from volcanic screed, ascending proved to be extremely difficult, with every step an increasing effort. The lactic acid burned deep in my legs and my chest heaved – even though I still hadn't touched a cigarette since Vietnam. I did feel like this mountain would beat me, but then I thought 'no way will I stop, I will climb this and beat it.' Taking a breather, looking around the magnificent views, I began to think how this trip had many peaks and troughs and one or two steep learning curves of its own, just like the mountain below my feet. Just when I thought I couldn't go any further, there had always been a light that guided me. So, I turned around, refocused and climbed it, no problem. It took around an hour and a half to get to its summit. It was well worth it though. Aside from the quite breath-taking views of the surrounding mountains, it was amazing to gaze into the mouth of a volcano. That lunch break was so sweet and my food tasted so good.

I then finished the rest of the stunning eight and a half hour tramp in style. Unfortunately I arrived half an hour late to catch my bus back to the village. Taking my bollocking from the local bus driver turned mountain guide like a man and jumping onto his bus instead, I thought; Stuff it, my mojo has returned.

***

"14.00 hours? Yes, that's okay, he says. Yep, he'll be there. Righty, goodbye then."

It was as simple as that. At 09.30 hours in my backpackers lodge, my free-fall tandem skydive had been arranged for this afternoon. All I had to do was drive from here to Lake Taupo. I had been desperate to do this bit of adrenaline rush since arriving in New Zealand and now, there it was, booked. I began to wish it wasn't.

Arriving at the bright yellow hangar next to Taupo's airport, it wasn't long before I was sitting with four other willing volunteers having the 'menu' of what to expect read out to us. I chose the 15,000ft jump with the photo and DVD package add on options. Before I had chance to say; 'Shit, what the fuck am I doing' and change my mind, I was led into the dressing-up area and given my helmet, goggles and bright red jump suit. Again, before I could say 'Can I just go for a piss?' Freddy, my Austrian jump-master was dancing around me, snaking perilously close to my vital areas as he deftly put me into my leg and shoulder harness. Already I could feel my nerves going a little, the anticipation filling me with a combination of fear and cold sweat.

'You have nothing to fear, Phil,' Freddy said in his distinct Austrian accent, the smell of stale tobacco blowing from his mouth up into my nostrils.

'I do all the work, you just enjoy, yes? My oldest jumper was 90 and my youngest 4, you have nothing to worry about, just relax and enjoy."

'It's that simple, is it, Freddy?' I thought. 'Okay, whatever.'

Thirty minutes later, the safety briefing over, one last nervous wave for the camera and that was it, the point of no return. Into the plane went five virgin jumpers, five skydivers, five cameramen and of course, the pilot came along as well. And up into the air we went.

The noise of the plane was deafening. As we gained height circling above Lake Taupo, the views on this beautiful day were absolutely stunning. In this near cloudless sky you could see for miles, or you could if you weren't busy clasping your hands together in prayer, staring at the floor, thinking 'what if.' Well, to be honest by now all I could think of was - exactly how does 15,000feet up in the air look? Sure, I'd been up in hundreds of planes on one flight or another, but how many of us really know where 15,000 feet actually sits in the sky? Bloody high is the only answer on that one. On the side of the plane an altimeter showed how far we'd climbed so far. At five thousand feet I would have quite happily jumped from that, it was high enough for me, but no, only another ten thousand more to go before we reached our jump height. I looked down, my sphincter muscle twitching uncomfortably, not even daring to emit a sly fart. I wouldn't have wanted to push that one.

Suddenly, without warning, my furry hat was planted firmly down onto my head, my goggles were fitted and the straps holding my jump-master and myself were pulled even tighter, pulling me back and sitting me onto Freddy's lap. A bit too close, or could we maybe class it as comfortable?

With the correct height now reached, the cabin light turned to green, the shutter rolled up with a loud crash and the wind filling the cabin howled like a banshee around us, slapping me across the face like a wet kipper. One pair at a time made their way to the exit door. Nervous smiles and shit poses for the static - extra money making, not included in the package - camera later, it was our turn. With a rather quick, forced smile after the flash went off, a shimmy to the front and one, two, threeee... a quick roll and Freddy threw us out into the sky.

I had never been so petrified in all my life. The first ten seconds felt like minutes as we tumbled and rolled over and over again, my face feeling like a crisp wrapper in a hurricane, the wind was slapping it that hard, the cold air biting into my ankles. Then I suddenly felt a tap on my arms. Time to take them off the straps, that's what he'd said in the briefing - "When I tap you, release your arms."

Not fucking likely.

The tap appeared again. 'Go away' was my first thought but this time, rather gingerly, I did unfold my arms. Below me the sky and the ground seemed to become one, an indistinct blur somewhere in the distance. I glanced all around, and saw about six feet below our cameraman with his camera pointing at me, waving madly like a drunk on a Saturday night piss up. I made a face, I put my thumbs into the diver's okay signal, and then I began to relax. After all, what the bloody hell else could I do? This had cost money and I was damn well going to enjoy it.

I thought of the inspirational Jack Nicholson and Morgan Friedman film 'The Bucket List' and how they did a skydive. Another one ticked off for me then, except this wasn't really my bucket list, this was my celebrating life and living in the moment list, or to put it even more succinctly, my 'fuck it' list. Suddenly, from nowhere my testicles moved from their tightly anchored place and hit me on the back of my head as Freddy pulled the rip cord. 60 seconds of free-fall had ended and suddenly it felt like a reverse bungee jump as we both shot back up into the sky at an amazing speed. Just what I'd expected I didn't know but my God, the adrenaline shot in, and I literally felt as free as a bird, indeed by now I really was 'Soaring with Eagles,' a feeling that was both amazing and exhilarating.

Freddy controlled our descent, swinging and pulling the cords left and right, twisting and turning into the thermals. It was like being on some kind of mad aerial roller-coaster ride. I howled and whooped with sheer joy as I couldn't believe how I could be up here in the clouds like this. I launched a million and one expletives and references to how amazed and overjoyed I was in Freddy's direction, although many disappeared into the air before they reached his ears. Just then my heart jumped a beat, as he decided to 'just loosen the straps off a bit, so we could land,' he said.

Well, if at any time I had thought that my life was literally in someone else's hands, now was that time. For a man who liked to be in control of his life, I literally felt like a puppet on a string. I had no control whatsoever, I had to have faith in the man pulling the strings, the man who had jumped a million times before and the man who would hopefully bring us safely back to earth. We landed safely of course, I did fall and land on my

arse, which was to be expected, but by now I could barely talk. The feeling enclosing me was one of total euphoria. My heart and my testicles felt like they were the wrong way round, blood pumped around my body with such force it felt like I'd completed the world's greatest Ironman contest. But what bloody good fun it was.

Driving off up to Rotorua about half an hour after landing probably wasn't a good idea as the lovely lady in the campsite reception found out to her cost. When I checked in I found I had come down with verbal diarrhoea and couldn't stop talking at her. That's adrenaline for you.

I planned to stay here for two nights on the camp site before driving to Mount Maunganui, then up towards Whitianga on the Coromandel. All steady away there really. After two nights sightseeing - but not bothering to stick my arse in the 'hot water beach' - I decided to not go any further north as my time in New Zealand was coming to an end, so I headed back towards the South Island again. Driving to the small town of Raglan, I met a lovely older woman in the I-site. We shared stories of travel and why I was here. When I told her that I was searching for something but didn't know quite what, she said that all we needed was to be happy, contented, and fulfilled. How true; once again the fundamentals of life and the words of wisdom that I probably needed to hear at that point sang out like a skylark on his morning call. I'd had a great time here in New Zealand, I knew that when the time came, I would be sad to leave. It had been a great test for me. I'd met some great people and got over the six month blip of travelling alone too. I've kept focused and had the strength not to give up. I have to keep remembering that. After all, that is the job of the lion on my shoulder isn't it, to provide that strength?

In the remainder of my time on North Island, a visit to the amazing Waitomo Caves was a definite highlight. How awesome do you think it would be to abseil 100 feet down through a gap less than the size of a manhole cover into the abyss below, to end up in a series of two million year old underground caves? I loved it, especially crawling through water and small gaps like some sort of Indiana Jones character. After the usual tramping around various chambers and jumping from a platform onto a tyre in a freezing underground river, our guide encouraged us to bang our tyres on top of the freezing water as hard as we could to wake up the glow-worms hanging from the roof of the cave above. I think we did more than wake them; we must have thoroughly pissed them off too, because they lit our way through the cavern, like turning on the house lights after a concert. It was an awesome sight. Being down there made me think of what it must be like to be trapped in a hole, unable to find your way out then suddenly, a light appears from nowhere and you move forwards with renewed vigour and confidence. A little bit like times in our lives really, no matter how hard things appear, there is always light at the end of the tunnel.

Five hours later, freezing cold and back on terra firma, I did get some suspicious looks when we got on the bus taking us back to our start point. I absolutely stank of piss. Now come on, hands up those who haven't weed in their wetsuits at some point? Yes, thought so, but I stank so bad I should have had a bell around my neck. I tried to hide it the best I could but Christ, it did smell bad. Luckily, I hadn't been the only one with this problem as another chap owned up - so the scent, so to speak, was deflected from me.

***

Driving south through the North Island, I passed all the places mentioned in William Pike's book, Mount Ruapehu where he lost his leg, and everywhere else which served either his rescue or recovery. I started to almost feel what he must have gone through that night. His book, like Lance Armstrong's, has served as a constant reminder of how strong the human spirit can be when under pressure. Travelling has allowed me to connect more strongly with my inner self and open my mind much further. On more than one occasion, I've found myself both tearful and humbled by reading and connecting with other people's life experiences. This has made me become so much more sensitive to my mortality and my own purpose in life. This, in turn, has allowed me to question the reasons why we are living the lives we are and consider how we can make whatever changes are needed to simplify them, rewarding not just ourselves but those around us too.

With an interview lined up for Friday, my time here had been spent constructively as there was a strong possibility two job opportunities would be on the table by the time I return to UK. Whether I would take them or not, I wasn't sure.

***

Returning to Christchurch, where it all started some nine weeks previously, I had two issues to deal with before leaving for Melbourne in four days time. The first was the interview which I'd now found out would not be on Friday, but on Monday morning, the day of my flight. Secondly, and perhaps more importantly, I needed to sell my car. Simple? No it wasn't, it was much harder than I'd thought it would be. Who wants to buy a car with 406,000km on the clock? No one it seemed.

The final day in New Zealand started positively enough. I had an interview with the Correctional Services and over an hour and a half later, was offered a job, subject to immigration clearance. That was a result in itself, but driving back to Christchurch, I thought to myself, why would I want to move 15,000 miles to take up a job I'd began to hate in the UK? It didn't make sense. But, for now, I would leave that offer open, pleased that I'd got something should I need it in the future.

Then came the next part of a long day. As it was the back end of the summer season, it was one hell of a struggle to sell the Red Shed. I'd had various tyre kickers and crappy enquiries from people who probably had absolutely no intention of buying the car. Eventually though I did sell it - at 5 o'clock in the evening, an hour before I had to leave for the airport. It certainly made me think about not leaving things like selling a car till the last minute again.

The Red Shed's new 17 year old owner had certainly bought himself a great car with almost as many memories as it had miles on the clock, although it did have a slightly dodgy gearbox! Sod it, for $1200NZ or 600 quid what do you want? I only lost $300NZ or 150 quid on what I'd paid for it, so a good result all round I thought. I hadn't needed anything flash or expensive and the car certainly wasn't anything fancy to look at, but it had been reliable, nice to drive and, other than the time with the dodgy alternator, it had not let me down. I actually felt sad to let it go.

Saying goodbye to Julia and Justin, I thanked them for their fantastic hospitality. I'd stopped with them twice now, at the beginning and now at the end of my time in New Zealand. For them to invite me into their home and let me come and go as I please and use all the facilities, shows how trust, respect and building up solid relationships can pay dividends.

By now I had a rough plan together for my time in Australia. I would be volunteering on a 4,000 acre cattle ranch east of Melbourne, Victoria before travelling to Adelaide and then to Alice Springs. A month later I would be flying onto Bali, teaching English at an after school club there.

I boarded the plane, sat back in my seat and looked out of the window, thinking about all the wonderful memories I'd had of this beautiful country over the past nine weeks. I felt pleased, two job offers open, meeting some lovely, genuine people and two worthwhile voluntary projects, it had certainly been one hell of a ride and now with two more lined up I felt proud of what I'd achieved and looked forward to what was to come next.

As Hannibal Smith used to say to the rest of the A Team; 'I love it when a plan comes together.' Now, it seemed, it was.

11
Treasure Island

I had visited Australia once before, some five years ago, just before I met my wife. On that occasion I travelled up the East coast experiencing the delights of Sydney, Newcastle, Brisbane and Steve Irwin's Australia Zoo, sailing around the Whitsunday Islands and diving on the Great Barrier Reef, the highlights on what had overall been a great trip. This time around things were planned out quite differently - not as much sightseeing, instead another voluntary work project intertwined with exploring other parts of this amazing and diverse country. I would be concentrating on Melbourne in the state of Victoria, before heading west to visit the central parts of this vast island.

I spent my first two nights in a grotty backpackers in the heart of downtown Melbourne before boarding a train bound for the town of Stratford, 220kms east of Melbourne, near the end of the Bairnsdale line, in the middle of Gippsland country. Stratford, like many of the towns and cities of Australia, took its name from its British counterpart. Wherever I looked there were references to the immortal bard - but that was where the similarity ended. The Aussie Stratford was lovely in its own right, although it would be fair to say it didn't enjoy any of the same cultural and historical delights as its UK counterpart.

I was heading for another voluntary project arranged through 'Workaway,' this time at a 4,000 acre cattle farm 5km from town. I was met at the railway station by the enthusiastic, and beautifully named, Mary Treasure.

As we headed towards her farm, I noticed the sign 'Homelands' by the gate as the car turned off the highway and swept up the drive towards the farm house. It was exactly what I'd imagined a typical Australian ranch home would look like - with an abundance of beef cattle, walers and other horses in the paddocks and kelpie sheep dogs running to great the 'ute' as its tyres crunched on the gravel. Once we'd unloaded the groceries, the welcome that Mary and her family gave me made me think that this would be a really good place to spend some quality time as a volunteer. I would be putting my joinery skills to good use too, renovating a cottage into a proposed holiday let. I would also be helping with beef cattle farming and various other farm works when needed.

What a great feeling this lovely place gave me. That night, along with the friends of the family also staying there, two Swedes named Felicia and Ben, I had a lovely dinner and a welcoming glass of 'goon'- the Aussie name for a box of cheap wine. It was at this time that the terms of my stay were explained. For the next ten days I would be given bed and food in return for working eight hour days in this beautiful location. I'm not much of a city boy, much preferring the peace and tranquillity of being at one with nature. This place was ideal, perfect even. I'd always wanted to work on a farm and being able to work on a project so beneficial and rewarding made the appeal all the more sweeter. After the ten weeks of the 'not stopping still for a minute' pace of New Zealand, ten days spent here would be just what the doctor ordered.

The commitment, effort, time and sheer determination Mary put into running the farm on a daily basis was both immediately noticeable and incredibly admirable, to say the least. The resilient Mary was Treasure by name and by nature. She had become a widow only five months ago. After a short illness, her husband Doug had succumbed to cancer. With four of her children and step children living away, it was mainly left to her and her daughter, Kate, to run the farm - with help, as and when needed, from neighbours and friends. I was quick to notice that since her husband died she was obviously finding things difficult. What she had been through and what she'd had to take on since, combined with the love effortlessly radiating from her beautiful and kind nature, made me all the more determined to give my time and help as best I could. That night, I tried to grasp the concept of what was happening here and how the next ten days would pan out. I needn't have worried, this place was indeed a real 'Treasure' and the very next morning, head thick with goon, I set to work with Ben and started on the renovation project of the cottage.

The cottage was well over a hundred years old and in a poor state internally. It had been built mainly from Red Gum, an Australian hardwood better known as eucalyptus, an excellent timber that had been used for centuries in building construction. This had been a project that had started some years earlier, yet never completed, mainly due to Doug's illness. Mary had wanted to eventually turn the cottage into a holiday let, gaining additional income to support the farm. As for me, I saw it as a way of helping a family that had suffered the loss of the head of that family. It was also a chance to bring my joinery skills out of retirement.

The cottage had a sitting tenant, the delightful, happy drunk and part-time farmhand, Geoffrey. He would often stay in bed whilst we knocked hell out of his living room and kitchen, eventually putting in an appearance mid-morning, nursing a hangover and breathing almost pure alcohol into the atmosphere. His cure, more often than not, was to open the fridge and take out another can of his favourite Jack Daniels and coke. He was a constant source of amusement, very knowledgeable and helpful - and he made my time here all the more enjoyable, even though his breath was strong enough to strip the paint off just about anything.

***

As the week progressed, I concentrated on the task in hand and helped out on the farm. By doing so, I found straight away that my focus, sense of purpose, self-belief and self-confidence had begun to rise again. I had realised something about myself too, that I cannot be put into a box. By that I mean I no longer viewed myself as a Senior Officer and manager in the Prison Service, a carpenter and joiner, a traveller or even a writer. I didn't need to be 'pigeon holed' to feel complete as a person. Okay, my true sense of purpose has not yet appeared, but I was now happier within, able to cope better with whatever life threw at me, more connected to the earth, more sensitive and aware of other people's needs, more grounded even. I haven't smoked for 3 months now and I'm finding more inner peace - although I can still get angry when I think of certain people or places from my past. Above all though, I've learned to accept what happened with my marriage. Deep down I know that Gemma has moved on now, living with someone else I believe, and I needed to do exactly the same thing - move on. If I take just one thing back at the end of this incredible year then it would be that. I have moved on. Now I believe that I can do anything I choose to put my mind to. I no longer have any self doubts about my strengths, weaknesses and abilities. I have embraced them all and, above all else, learned to love who I am and what I have to offer to the world. I could sense that something amazing was going to happen soon - but what, I wonder?

I enjoyed my time on the Treasure Farm. The weather was still glorious as autumn set in; Cricket, the farmhouse Jack Russell dog, provided a much needed source of amusement and entertainment, and each day started with a brew and breakfast. I passed the evenings in the farmhouse, talking and putting the world to rights over a glass of goon - which actually wasn't as bad as it sounds - or stoking the fire in the farmhouse annexe which had become home. I also enjoyed whiling some of the evenings away with Ben. Even though we worked all day together, his dry humour was a constant source of amusement. Felicia was fun too; only 20, she was a previous volunteer who had had a dreadful accident on a horse and badly broken her ankle. Mary had let her stay as long as she wanted to and, being really good friends with Kate, the arrangement worked well. Still in a supportive boot some 3 months after her accident, Homelands proved to live up to its name at this frustrating point in her life. Just sitting watching her and Kate chatting about the usual rubbish on TV cheered me up no end.

I felt settled, enjoying a purpose to my travels once more and the company was lovely. I couldn't help but admire Mary. Even though she was over 60 years old, she would throw herself into every aspect of farm life with amazing passion, throwing bales of hay around like they were nothing.

As the week progressed into the next, so did the work on the cottage. One job after another was finished. Even the plasterer had been in and worked his magic by the time it came for me to say farewell. The cottage was fast approaching completion and I felt extremely proud of my efforts. This had been a superb voluntary project with more than one reward as, not only had I enjoyed the opportunity to do some quality work, I'd also been welcomed into a lovely family. I'd also managed to ride one of the beautiful chestnut coloured walers, de-horn cattle, do a little bit of droving and repair fences along the way.

On the last night I sat up in bed, reflecting on the past ten days. I had been invited into the Treasure family and treated like one of their own; I'd rebuilt a cottage and thoroughly enjoyed the experience of working on this 4000 acre farm, so much so that I was in two minds about leaving. I had to do so, I realised that, but feeling so settled and valued again made it all the more difficult.

The next day, as Mary dropped me off at the railway station, there was time for one last surprise to hit me. As I lifted my rucksacks out of the trunk, we chatted about what we had both gained from this experience. Then, suddenly, she handed me a folded envelope.

"Here's a little something for you," she said. "It's for all your hard efforts."

My first reaction was one of surprise. I looked at the brown envelope. I didn't want to take it but she was insistent. I had been fed and sheltered admirably and in return I had worked every day - and diligently too. It was hard to repay that kindness alone, so why was she giving me an envelope?

"I don't know what to say, Mary," I replied, guessing that it would probably contain money, though at the same time keeping my fingers crossed, hoping it didn't contain tickets to a Cliff Richard concert.

"You've worked so hard; treat yourself to something - something to remember us all by," she said, obviously meaning every word.

Stunned and completely overwhelmed, I could feel a lump rising in my throat. It rose even further when, an hour or so into my train journey to Melbourne, curiosity got the better of me. I opened the envelope to discover it contained $250. I knew this trip would offer me penitence on more than one occasion, but to be given a gift like this, I was shocked, yet extremely grateful at the same time.

I arrived in Melbourne, alone again but happy. Grabbing an awful burger meal at 'Hungry Jacks,' I noticed a mouse staring up at me as I ate it, probably wondering if one of his family was between the bread bun.

Then it was time to pick up my hire car, a crappy little Nissan Micra. I spent the next five days having some fun driving it along the Great Ocean Road, up into Halls Gap, through the Grampians National Park into Adelaide - a journey of some 900km. There was certainly some stunning scenery along the way, such as the 12 Apostles natural rock formation. Getting up close to kookaburras and koala bears in their natural environments was great and Halls Gap village had breath-taking views to rival any National Park I'd visited. It also had some of the cutest, yet destructive, kangaroos as visitors.

Staying in hostels along the way there was plenty of time to think about my future; what would my long term plan be; what would I do? I couldn't make any long term decision at all. In the end, I decided to look at focusing on the next twelve months; I would walk the Camino as planned, and publish the book you're now reading.

If I were to be perfectly honest with myself, deep down I knew I didn't want to live in the UK permanently. After eight long months travelling, I now know what I do not want in my life. When we are moving on from something negative, just how we deal with overcoming the hurdle comes to the very forefront of our mind with every thought. As I've said before, my career had been turned into a mundane, predictable job that neither stimulated nor invigorated me. But now I realised that, after twenty-five years of being an employee, I couldn't work for anyone anymore; now I wanted complete freedom and control over my decisions and destiny. This time away from my comfort zone had raised my game considerably, improving my self-confidence and belief in my own abilities. Another thing I've noticed is that what previously would have been major talking points have now become trivial matters - mountains have become molehills. I can do anything I want to do in life, I just have to plan, prepare and take decisive action. I really don't care about what others think, it's not selfish, but at this stage, I only have to satisfy myself.

****

I arrived in Adelaide for an overnight stop before joining a 'Groovy Grape' trip to Alice Springs - six days and five nights of what amounted to a glorified 'boys own adventure.' The bus had 18 backpackers on board from every corner of the globe. With Steve, the slightly nuts but amazingly knowledgeable tour guide at the wheel, I sensed that this could be a great trip and a different way to see unchartered parts of Australia.

Whether this trip would be one to remember would be largely dependent on the 'group dynamics,' as it is on any trip like this. By the time we rolled into Alice Springs, it had certainly been one to remember - and quite fondly at that. Every day we would all muck in and help prepare the 'bush tucker,' then we'd all work as a team, wash up and load the bus, ready for the next part of the adventure. Well, apart from 'Team Taiwan' who not only failed to grasp the concept of teamwork, but also had the physical work ethics of someone half dead.

On our way we explored the breath-taking scenery of the Flinders Ranges National Park. Each night we slept by a roaring camp fire in 'swags' - a combined mattress, sleeping bag and waterproof exterior shell, an essential bit of kit for every Bushman. The only exception being when we visited the slightly crazy and potentially inbred opal mining town of Coober Pedy where the night was spent sleeping in an underground cave. It is so hot there, that many years ago the locals decided to build their houses underground where the temperature is a steady 27 degrees all year round. The morning after, as we left our underground hostel, Steve decided to casually drop in the fact that ghostly noises had regularly been heard, seemingly coming out from the cave walls, and that 'orbs' had appeared quite often on photographs taken there. Sure enough, after some of the ladies of the group stopped screaming hysterically, there was the evidence on Sarah's camera. There were none on mine, nor on others, but the large spotted circles were very clear on hers. Orbs are thought by many, including myself, to be the first stage of a spirit manifestation. Spooky or what? Strange but true.

From Coober Pedy, the bus snaked along the desert highway towards the Northern Territory and the jaw dropping Uluru - better known as Ayers Rock. This stunning red rock in the middle of nowhere invites tourists from all over the world to get up at a ridiculous hour and freeze whilst waiting for the sun to come up, bathing the rock in a red glow.

It was here that I chatted with Sarah, a nice Yorkshire lass whose company I'd enjoyed on board the bus. She was also on a journey of self discovery and awakening. Bored, and with a mundane job, she'd split from her boyfriend which made her look at what changes she wanted to make in her life. Frustrated with a lack of clear focus and direction, she was travelling around Australia and New Zealand, hopeful of new doors opening. But what?

How many of us feel like this? Life is too short to think of limiting the untapped power and potential we all have within ourselves. The Lance Armstrong cancer survival book I'd read highlighted the fact that sometimes the shit in our lives is good for us; it provides balance, heightening our awareness and appreciation of the good times when they come around, helping to keep our feet firmly on ground.

We spent another night at Uluru and the nearby Kata Tjuta before trekking through the quite amazing Kings Canyon. By the end of the tour we'd covered 2200km in six days. I'd bonded with some nice people, improved my German phrases and learnt some new swear words. We arrived, ready to stay overnight in Alice Springs before having to turn around and travel the whole bloody distance back to Adelaide, this time on a Greyhound bus that would take around 16 hours.

For me, sleeping in swags in the open air proved to be a highlight of this trip. There's nothing quite like being tucked up in these amazingly comfortable contraptions, gazing up at the Southern Cross and the many other constellations visible on a crisp, clear autumn evening. I really did feel close to nature lying in one of these; in fact on the last night, maybe a little too close. The following morning the crazy Steve told us that a pack of dingo's had been foraging around our camp in the early hours, passing only feet away from our sleeping bodies.

As I prepared to spend the night in Alice Springs, it crossed my mind that I could have planned this better. From here I could have taken another trip north to Darwin and flown to Bali from there. Instead I was making my way back to Adelaide where I would be spending a few days high up in the Williamstown area of the Barossa Valley, with a lovely couple I'd met in Vietnam.

***

When I arrived at my friends, I'd not been there more than a couple of hours before my upbeat mood took a massive hit. I checked my emails, only to read that a friend of mine, Adam Robinson, had died. I was devastated by this sad news. Over the couple of years I'd known him, we had become friends. We were both the same age and with music and one thing and another, we'd had a lot in common. I'd done some coaching sessions with him, and he was a really nice and genuine man. He was an instrument builder and repairer, and a very talented one at that. He'd done a superb job repairing my electric guitar - that's how I first met him.

He'd become ill just before Christmas, though he didn't know what was wrong with him, believing it was something with his liver or kidneys. Now, just a short time later, he had succumbed to cancer.

Adam was divorced with an eight year old son. Thinking back to the last time I saw him, I remembered the conversation we'd had as we shared a cup of coffee - only four days before I flew out to Sri Lanka.

"Life's short," he had said. "We need to do what we can, see what happens and don't regret what you're doing; you'll have a great time."

With those words echoing around my mind, I was once again reminded of how poignant they had become. Life is indeed so short, yet maybe we still don't embrace it like we should and push ourselves into doing as much as we can with the opportunities we have - and learn from every lesson given.

I'm learning to live every day to the full, embrace change, take chances, grasp new opportunities and look for any way to enrich and develop myself as a person. I'd discovered the need to simplify my existence and clear out unwanted hassle from my everyday life and, above all, to enjoy the life I am fortunate to have been blessed with.

Being 11,000 or so miles away from family and friends at a time like this made me realise all the more just how important it is to value and cherish every moment of every day - and the special people in our lives too - as we never know what is around the corner. It also made me look at my own life, thinking:- 'Well, life's really not that bad, I have wonderful family and friends, and I can tell them that when I next see or speak to them.' Adam doesn't have that opportunity anymore and there's an eight year old boy who now has no father figure, a guiding light to inspire him. Cancer has taken that away from him.

As I fought the lump in my throat, I now became even more determined to walk the Camino de Santiago in his and every other sufferers' memory.

Perhaps this news was another wake up call to who I truly am, what I am about and the message I can give to other people. I realise now, more than ever, that we must look inside ourselves and see that we should never take anything in life for granted and live life to our fullest potential. Maybe we should all try harder to eliminate any negativity from our lives, decide what we want and don't want and then deal with it. We need to be looking at what makes us happy and change what doesn't. It infuriates me when we end up doing work that drags us down beneath the level we should be at and live boring, mediocre lives because of it.

Peter, one of the friends I was staying with in Adelaide, wasn't happy and wanted to change something in his life but his current job underpins everything in it, yet it undermines everything else of importance. Only he can change it; the question is, once he knows what he needs to look at, has he got the strength to do so?

***

I spent a great couple of days exploring the wonderful Barossa Valley wine country around Adelaide. The German winemaker Wolf Blass liked the climate, soil and the variety of grape so much, he moved down here and built a bloody big factory. The next day and the Cleland Wildlife Park, home to some of

Australia's iconic animals, proved to be more beneficial than I thought it would be. There I was able to hand feed rescued or rehabilitated kangaroos and wallabies and hold a koala bear too. How amazing is that? Only a couple of weeks earlier I'd been running around trying to photograph koalas in the wild, so to have my photo taken actually holding one was absolutely priceless. They really are as cute and cuddly as they look and feel incredibly like a kid's toy. I loved snuggling the little fella; it really was one of those magic moments. After all, we rarely get to opportunity to engage with wildlife like this. Thinking back to my time as a Pets as Therapy volunteer, I remembered how stroking the volunteers' pets really cheered up the hospital's patients. And now this little chap was cheering me up. Animals have an uncanny ability to heal us.

***

Before long it was time to leave the hills of Adelaide and head back to Melbourne. Whilst there, I treated myself to a new pair of trainers with Mary's money. Being on the road and walking as much as I had, I'd worn out a pair of trainers and a pair of hiking boots, so it seemed a good idea to invest in something to remember the Treasure farm by.

I felt a little apprehensive about being on my own again but that was just my comfort zone being kneaded into shape once more. All I was doing was 'tuning into it.' Still, when you travel alone you don't know quite what to expect - but you have to keep going. By this stage I'd extended my flight back to the UK by six weeks and now found myself entering June and the final two months of the trip.

Nearly 9 months had passed since I first left the UK, heading off into the sunset looking for adventure, for the changes that I'd wanted to make in my life and for new opportunities to grace my future. In the beginning, when everything went tits up in Sri Lanka, time seemed to last forever. Since then time had rushed forward in a heady mix of sun, fun, voluntary work and quite amazing countries, leaving me now thinking about every last bloody second of it.

What would happen when I went back to the UK, I wondered? It had crossed my mind on more than one occasion. The one thing that I wanted more than anything was not to tread the same pathways, repeating the pattern that I'd been so determined to change in the first place. So, what would my plan be when this bubble of travel ended? Unfortunately this was now an impending reality and had to be faced. And what did I decide? Well, firstly the house has to go; deep down I'd known that a long time ago. I can't hang onto something that holds me back. Besides, it's only bricks and mortar, nothing that important. Secondly I'll move back to Bury, well, I think I will, and thirdly I'll definitely walk the Camino. And after that..? Fuck knows.

If nothing else, one thing I have learnt from this trip is not to think and plan like I had in the past. Of course it is important to be aware of the future but, with other things to think through first, sometimes the statement 'do nothing and live today' comes to mind. Maybe something else will materialise first. Who knows? let's enjoy the ride while it's here. Leaving Australia comes first.

So what would transpire from here? Would I come across another opportunity of some sorts? A new girlfriend perhaps? Would I enjoy even more magical experiences, ones that could never be erased from the memory bank? Would I help make a difference to those in need, wherever in the world they may be? I had no idea; only the next couple of months would tell.

12
The Return of the Bum Gun

Waking up to the sound of children singing is always a nice feeling; it reminds me of carol services at Christmas. Opening my eyes, I reached for my watch, checked the time and looked around the room to remind myself of where I was. After three and a half months away, I was in South Eastern Asia again, this time in Bali, Indonesia. Opening the door, I breathed in the familiar, pure, unpolluted air of an Asian countryside. From the patio outside my villa, I looked across the open fields. In every direction I could see lush, green grass, palm trees and plants. I could see the thatched roofs of buildings against a backdrop of a pure, blue sky filled with exotic birds in flight. As skinny looking chickens pecked at the stone ground, hopeful of finding something to eat, from somewhere in the distance I heard the faint rumbling of passing traffic. Back in my room, ants were marching on the table and floor, and geckos were running amok on the ceiling and walls. Taking all of this in, I thought what pure and special moments these really are, ones to be cherished and enjoyed. Another day in paradise - my home for the next two weeks or so.

I'd arrived at Slukat Learning Centre in Bali, Indonesia, where I'd be teaching English to children of varying ages and levels. One of the things that had attracted me to voluntary teaching here was the fact that it provided free after school education for the children from Keramas village, Gianyar town and the surrounding areas.

Founded in 2007 by Agung Rai and Ayu Darsini, with a belief that education was the most valuable gift they could give, their vision was to provide the children with a better future. The centre supports the children's basic schooling in neighbouring towns with extra English classes and computer skills from Monday to Thursday, 15.30 through to 18.30. There were also recycling and organic farming programs here, aiming to educate and raise awareness in all the students. Around fifty students visited Slukat each day, their ages ranging from 8-20 years, most coming from local farming or low income families. Three times a week there was also a morning day care class for 3-5 year olds.

The centre relies on native English speakers to volunteer and help the children as much as they can. The interaction with people from other countries and cultures helps to build the children's character and develop their self-confidence. Since its doors first opened five years ago, more than eighty volunteers of fifteen nationalities have helped to make a difference to the future education, careers and lives of these young people. Impressive really, I thought, and something I'd find to be very beneficial too.

For a small weekly fee of around £90 for accommodation, a basic breakfast and evening meal on school days, it really gave me the opportunity to embrace the Balinese culture in its entirety.

With the arrival gates of Manchester Airport's Terminal One looming, this would probably be my last volunteering opportunity of this trip, so I was keen to make it a bloody good one. I was really looking forward to teaching again. Recently, on parts of the journey in Australia, I'd occasionally become a little downhearted and despondent. I'd realised that this was not due to boredom but because I had nothing to focus on. Sure, I'd thrown myself into the joinery project on the Treasure farm and had a great experience but, since then, I'd travelled solo for nearly three weeks which had felt soulless at times, despite the riches gained from every new person I'd met and every experience I'd had. By this time I had, on occasion, felt fed up with travel even though, deep down, I knew I actually wasn't. I guess I was suffering from the 'loneliness of the long distance runner' syndrome. Hopefully though, dropping anchor here for two to three weeks would help.

After the rush of Australia, I was looking forward to slowing things down a little and rewinding the clock back to the pace I'd become so used to in Asia. Here in Bali, the love from the predominantly Hindu people radiates not only in their voice, but also in their gentle and caring nature. But then, there is the other side to Asia, with things that don't work, are broken or just not there in the first place. Though this is rather annoying, it's all part of Asia's charm. My shower didn't work properly, my room was full of ants and nothing that should have closed, did so. Aaah, the beauty of Asia. Still, problems are there to be solved, not moaned about. Best of all though, I had been reunited with an old friend - the bum gun! Thank God for small things, but important nonetheless.

It was a blissfully hot Monday morning and, after reporting to the office, I was shown around the centre and its facilities by the strange mannered and actually quite irritating, Vjara, an older lady who was allegedly the 'Volunteer Co-ordinator,' although I found her to be more obstructive than helpful. My first day consisted of shadowing five Dutch girls already here, giving me the chance to observe how they took the classes and see for myself the lessons given in the four classrooms. It also gave me the opportunity to introduce myself to some of the students I would be teaching. Quite strange really, but we don't give other nations enough credit sometimes. These girls were teaching English to students. Strange? Yes, because it's not their native tongue, yet they speak English so well. I'd noticed that most of the nationalities I'd encountered on my travels could speak English but how many of us in the UK can speak Dutch, German, French or Spanish? Too few of us. I can speak some German and actually enjoy learning and speaking new phrases but we do take the speaking of English by the rest of the world too much for granted.

After two days, having co-taken a class with a Dutch volunteer, I'd suddenly realised that travel with purpose and meaning was definitely the way forward. I felt re-energised and focused once more. For me, keeping active and busy helped no end and, by the end of the first week, I'd thoroughly enjoyed the experience of teaching English again. By and large, the children I taught here were like those in Cambodia and Thailand - nothing short of brilliant. Keen, and wanting to learn English, yet often shy and reserved, they were a real pleasure to teach. With the technique I'd developed in Surin, some truly inspired bits of improvisation and gentle coaxing of the shyest ones, the results were amazing. Shyness is a part of the Hindu culture that the children embrace, so patience is a factor to build in when planning lessons - but the rewards it brought when the children understood my efforts and showed their appreciation warmed my heart no end.

My final Thursday evening class of that first week gave me the most pleasure; my lesson planning and preparation, combined with the way I'd allowed the lesson to flow, gave the students a new found confidence in standing up and speaking. That one moment, seeing the smiles on the student's faces was priceless. The pleasure it gave me, knowing that my approach had worked, was, for me, like having a shot of an adrenaline drug.

I enjoy teaching; giving knowledge and acting as a positive role model to others is very rewarding. Yet, what these Hindu children teach us in return is also very important. The beginning of every lesson was, in accordance with Hindu tradition, opened with a prayer for protection and blessing. The end of the lesson is closed in the same manner. As the younger children leave the classroom, they hold your hand and place their forehead against it, as a sign of respect. This is so important to their culture - as is the position they hold within it. There are four castes within the Hindu religion and knowledge and understanding of how they work is fundamental in teaching the children. As I mentioned before, the children here don't get the education they so deserve unless they are able to pay for it, so to see their faces light up with every new word or phrase learnt is a joy to behold.

As time went by, I began to feel more and more comfortable with teaching; I was enjoying the experience, growing as a teacher and now starting to think about taking a paid position in China.

***

I still feel lonely and incomplete; I know there is a piece missing and I'm starting to get tired now and want to find peace. I thought about how I hadn't found love again or a clear direction in which to head. But, hang on, did I really expect to do so with moving around so much? Yes and no. There is a part of this soppy old twat that wants to have children, find a new direction and love. But maybe I have. I like teaching, so maybe I should go down that route? I need to think about things but not beat myself up in the process. Travelling has been one hell of a challenge; I've shown inner strength, resilience, faith, belief and understand others so much more than I thought I ever would. I've become much more tolerant, sensitive to the needs of others, compassionate and emotional. I'm realising that if I can overcome this year, then what else am I capable of achieving in the future? I know that I will have to focus on the Camino walk first. Maybe then I can find what I truly want from life. I'm still unclear of the direction to take but somehow feel that I am on the right pathway. Only time will tell, I guess.

***

After the first week's teaching was over, I decided to hire a rather fetching red moped so I could explore the roads of Bali on my weekend off. First I visited the cultural town of Ubud, where I watched the England Euro 2012 game against Sweden. As the game started at 2.45am I didn't get much sleep. In the morning, feeling like jet-lag had set in, I set off up towards Gunung Batur, an active volcano in North East Bali. It felt good to be out and about on the bike soaking in the atmosphere and sights on the journey north.

All was going well until, 5 kms from Batur, I encountered a police road check. Beckoned to join the polite, English speaking policeman, who looked remarkably like the one from the 'Village People', he struck up the usual 'where are you from?' conversation. Aware of what he was up to, I produced my UK driving licence and registration documents for the bike. After saying how good it was that I had a UK driving licence, he explained that there would be a 'fine' for not having an international or Balinese driving licence - which apparently I didn't need anyway.

"Should I pay the fine to you personally?" I asked.

"I can help you if you help me," he replied. In other words, how much of a bribe would I give him to let me go on my way? Holding out a 50,000IRD note, worth about £3.50, I discreetly placed it in his hand. When he told me that he wanted 250,000 IRD, I informed him of my professional position in the UK. That seemed to do the trick; he accepted the note and waved me good day.

I smiled as I had known exactly what these chaps were up to. A bribe here and there boosts their inadequate salary quite considerably. Still, at least it was a better outcome than I'd witnessed in Laos. That had annoyed me so much and my arse had twitched as I'd approached the road block. But, what I'd ridden into had been covered in Charley Boorman's and Ewan McGregor's 'Long Way' series. Thankfully I'd remembered what I'd read, so I knew how to deal with it. Spotting another quite pissed off 'western meal ticket' jumping back onto his bike, I asked him if he had been 'fined.' He had - but he'd had to pay 100,000 IRD.

Further up the road I bumped into two rather pleasant British ladies and we drove together down towards Besakih Temple, Bali's most important Hindu temple. There we were guided towards the 'Tourist Information Office' where we came across yet another scam. They tried to trick travellers into paying 450,000IRD, around £34, for a 'guide' which you categorically did not need. The Lonely Planet guide even mentioned how this angered and annoyed travellers. This time I wasn't having any of it but, taking a peek at their 'registration book,' it seemed this particular scam had reeled in more than one money paying fish today.

Leaving the lovely British girls, I continued to enjoy the freedom of riding the moped on the island's roads. This is what I like most in my life – freedom. Journeying on Bali's roads gives the opportunity to marvel at the life in the villages and towns you pass through. With palm trees lining each side of the road like spectators on the Tour de France, people toiling in the lush, green paddy fields on every side, barefoot children running around dressed in shirts and shorts with grins as big as Cheshire cats, shouting and waving at me and the men of the villages sitting outside their houses, fondly stroking their fighting cocks whilst other elder men glanced admiringly in their direction. Cock fighting is illegal in Indonesia, as it is in many countries; nevertheless it is still a popular pastime for males of all ages. What a great feeling to be seeing and absorbing all of this, particularly from a moped which gives the freedom to weave in and out of people's lives. Utterly priceless.

The standard of driving here is no better than in other parts of Asia, but at least the roads are quite good. Everywhere you see objects balanced precariously on un-roadworthy mopeds, families of four or five sitting on every bit of space there is, overtaking and undertaking. But I never witnessed any malice, swearing, gesticulating, or accidents.

***

Teaching alongside the Dutch volunteers had been okay but I often felt excluded - not in the 'clique,' so to speak. By the third week though, the clog-hoppers had gone, leaving behind a great mix of newly arrived Irish, British and Australian volunteers. Forming a great group dynamic, the last week was worth more than the first two put together. As my time teaching had progressed, I'd felt more and more comfortable, finding my own style and enjoying the interactions with every class. This would make it harder to pull away from this oasis of love, peace and harmony when my time here came to an end.

Waking up on my final day, I heard the sound of children talking and clapping. On making my way to breakfast I found some twenty children in the main hall rehearsing a dance routine for a camping trip in a couple of weeks' time. From maybe 7 years old to around 15, they were all concentrating on every step and move with so much enthusiasm and passion evident in their faces.

With just two lessons remaining before my time here came to an end, the first of these at 15.30, I prepared really good lesson plans before making the most of what free time I had.

That first lesson turned out to be probably the best one I'd done since coming here. The children as usual were keen to learn and the tricky subject of 'My Family' was finally hitting home. After an hour and a half, I felt a real sense of achievement as their vocabulary and pronunciation was so much better than when I'd first taken this class three weeks earlier.

After the second lesson had finished, all the children came to the main classroom and hall where, clapping and cheering, they presented me with my volunteer's certificate, reminding me of my final day in Thailand. I remembered how emotional I'd felt then and today was no different. I felt satisfied, strong, drained and, above all, proud. To give to others is one thing but here I didn't feel like it was a chore, it just felt right and without much effort too. How I wish the western world would adopt these core values, the world would be such a better and more loving place in an instant. It made it even more special when one of my older students told me what a good teacher I was and that she hoped that someday I'd return. Receiving comments like that is truly uplifting as it helps to make you feel all the more valued and appreciated.

That night became a little celebration of my time at Slukat. A few drinks to say goodbye to the new group of volunteers I'd bonded with felt like a good idea. I had a week or so of my 30 day visa left and I knew exactly where I would be heading from here - The Gili Islands.

Packing my rucksack that night, I found a pair of jeans and trainers that I no longer needed. When the next day dawned, holding them in my hand on my way to say goodbye to everyone, I passed the gardener who was the first person I'd met on my arrival. Always managing a smile through his two teeth, thin as a slate baton but with much love and kindness radiating, I instantly knew where these clothes were heading. Seeing that they would fit him, I offered him the trainers. Then the $15 jeans from the Op Shop in NZ also found their new owner – though I did think he'd probably need a belt. No verbal communication was needed, a gesture, a smile and finally a handshake and my good deed for the day was done.

After breakfast I said goodbye to all at Slukat Learning Centre, thanked them for a unique experience and set off along the coast to Padang Bai, destination, Gili Islands - a group of three islands, Gili Trewangan, Gili Meno and Gili Air, off the north west coast of Lombok. These islands prove to be a major draw for backpackers, families and travellers alike, mainly due to its environment and chilled out vibe, although the fact that mushrooms can be legally taken here, the only drug that is legal in Indonesia, may also be a reason for their popularity - though God only knows why people take mushrooms. As for myself, I was attracted to the sea and marine life which is absolutely stunning. Whatever the attraction, most people, myself included, opt for the fast boat crossing and stay on the biggest one of the three- Gili Trewangan. My intention there was to do nothing except chill and dive and that is precisely what I did.

What a great way to finish off the last week here. On the beach one day, I felt drawn to buying a simple gecko pendant from one of the beach vendors. Wondering why I was drawn to this simple yet striking design, the reason for my fascination soon dawned on me. Aside from great fun to watch, geckos are adaptable, flexible, enduring and loyal. They can climb any surface, a mountain even, and overcome challenges. Who did that remind me of? Me - though it could be any of us if we choose to acknowledge and recognise it. Snorkelling on the Gili islands also proved to be somewhat of a revelation with green turtles in abundance, often coming right onto the shore. I would spot two or three on each swim. How cool is that? I stayed for nearly a week here in the back of a dive shop and there was some great diving to be had on this tropical paradise - a nice way to end a memorable month on the island of Bali. Oh, with a few beers and some reggae music on a night too of course.

In fact, my time on the trip in general was summed up on a dive to Sunset Point, the day before I was due to fly up to Jakarta and then onto Kota Kinabalu in Malaysian Borneo. During a random chat with the South African dive master, we swapped tales of why we were both here and our journeys in the past. It turned out she had been fed up with life too and greeted me as a fellow 'fuck it person' - one abandoning a regular life in search of simplicity and authenticity.

The next day, sinking into my seat for the flight from Bali to Jakarta, I smiled as I remembered what she'd said. That was a statement and a half - and I liked it!

13
Crossing Borders

It has to be said that I've learned some pretty damn good things about myself over the past nine and a half months. And now, with only five weeks before Manchester Airport loomed again, how would the trip end? On a high note hopefully. I was now entering my ninth country and, with eight voluntary projects undertaken, I thought time just kicking back, chilling out and sightseeing would be time well spent. With that in mind, I thought long and hard about where to head for next. Having done most of South-East Asia, Australia and New Zealand, China looked a good bet but arranging a visa from here would have been a bloody nightmare. So, looking at my demographics, knowing that my return flight was from Kuala Lumpur, Borneo and Malaysia seemed like the best option.

Arriving late on Saturday evening, I'd checked into the wonderful Masada backpacker hostel in Kota Kinabalu and given myself a day or two to look around and decide what to see and do. One thing that seemed to be a good idea at the time was to climb the impressive Mount Kinabalu, one of Borneo's biggest tourist attractions. To climb all 4095 metres of it certainly is a challenge. Usually climbed over two days and involving staying at a ridiculously overpriced guesthouse halfway up the mountain until a quarter to three the next morning before ascending to the summit. Karl, a German traveller I'd met in the hostel, and I wondered if it could be done in a day, saving us a lot of money in the process. Asking other travellers, none had attempted to do it this way, all opting to pay through the nose to 'bag' the mountain. Being British and up for anything - legal of course - and Karl being German, thinking he could conquer the world, we decided between ourselves that yep, we could do it. There was of course, a small matter of remembering that eleven hours is a bloody long time to be hiking and climbing. After two days of planning we left our nearby guest house, had our permits stamped, picked up our guide and arrived at the Tymphon Gate starting point at 07.30am determined to climb this beast in a day.

Within an hour I was nearly blowing out of my arse. The going was relentless, and I mean relentless; my 'Icebreaker' merino wool top so wet I was frequently having to wring it out. After half an hour, Karl had sped off ahead, leaving me to climb with only Wilfred, our guide, for company. As he spoke little English, it became a lonely struggle upwards, one that soon turned from a hike into a full blown climb, each step heavier than the one before. I started brightly enough but by the time I hit the three hour point, I was physically shattered. Like a fool, after four months of not smoking, I'd started again in the Gili Islands and now I was paying for it. Karl was nowhere to be seen; maybe he was in a rush to put a towel down on the summit. In any case, there was serious doubt that I'd be able to get to the top before the cut off time of 1 o'clock when I would not be able to climb any further, mainly due to the time restrictions in place for day climbers. It would be dangerous and foolish to descend any later as it would take at least five hours to get back down.

On reaching the crucial stop of Laban Rata guest house, I afforded myself the luxury of a ten minute brew and butty break before Wilfred and I set off again on our push for the summit. As we resumed the climb, my legs would just not move. With each step feeling like I was wearing diver's boots, I was trying everything I could think of to motivate myself, talking to my subconscious, thinking positive thoughts - whatever I could really - but it was a long, hard, arduous slog, with each step becoming more and more difficult.

Progress was slow yet steady. With just 750 metres to go, I stopped for a chicken leg and a much needed breather. It was here that my mission ended. I looked at my watch and groaned; it was 12.45. Suddenly, Karl emerged from the mist, bounding back down from the summit like a mountain goat and grinning from his obviously successful mission to plant that towel on the top. By the time I'd unsuccessfully tried to communicate with Wilfred on whether or not we could climb any further, my mission was over. I was bitterly disappointed, everything I'd put into the hike seemed to have been in vain, but it was just too late in the day to go on any further.

To have come so near - and yet so far - was hugely disappointing and frustrating. I tried to convince myself that maybe it takes more courage to admit defeat and turn back rather than press on in search of a prize, which in this case would be just to be able to say I'd 'bagged' a mountain. To help lift my spirits, on the way back down I seized the chance to help improve young Wilfred's English. It didn't dispel my disappointment but helping him out did do a little to hide it. It took us five and a half hours to climb back down. In fact we were the last ones to leave, the park ranger clanging the gates shut behind us at half past six.

The next day my legs felt like lead weights, every last bit of energy completely sapped. The challenge had been immense but, on reflection, I felt good. Apart from being one hell of a work out, I'd almost achieved something else that so many people didn't think possible, and at my age too.

***

I'd started to become used to the idea that I'd be returning to the UK. Obviously I was looking forward to being re-united with family and friends. Without either, what are we? Mine are very important to me, so sharing a beer over a story or two and enjoying my mother's budget style cooking seemed a good idea. Being away for so long leads to re-evaluating what matters in life. Since being on the road, I've had news of two friend's father's fighting cancer along with losing a friend and discovering the news that my next door neighbour is battling with cancer too. When would it be my turn, I wondered? Or any of us for that matter. I've often thought about that. The awareness of our own mortality certainly becomes stronger as we age, but it also gives us the opportunity to re-evaluate our lives and challenge ourselves to live a better and higher life.

One of the things to help motivate me further had been another inspirational story I'd read - about Katie Piper, the beautiful British girl horribly disfigured when her ex-boyfriend arranged to have acid thrown in her face. I'd wept as I found her courage and her determination to fight her way back to health incredible and inspiring - despite her having over 100 operations with more to come. This book, along with those of Lance Armstrong and William Pike, proved to me beyond any doubt what the human spirit is capable of achieving. It is so powerful and can be used in such a positive way, for the good of humanity and mankind. When we read stories like theirs, our own problems, whinges and moans pale into complete insignificance, don't they?

***

Returning to the city of Kota Kinabalu, I had time to connect with some truly great people at the hostel before I decided to move on. One of those was Leo, a young, intelligent Tasmanian lad seemingly on a flat out mission to travel to as many places as he could in just three weeks. Over a couple of days our mutual bonds grew stronger as we shared our life experiences with each other. It must have been a trust thing, because, on a visit to the beautiful Tunku Abdul Rahman National Park, Leo felt comfortable enough to share with me that his father had, quite unexpectedly, hanged himself only five weeks previously. Leaving his mother and siblings back home, Leo had felt the urge to get away, not only to try to come to terms with his sad loss but also to look for answers to the questions spinning round madly in his head - 'Why?' being the obvious one. But would knowing the answer make it any easier to deal with? 'No' is the simple answer to that one. Only time could possibly heal him. When situations like these arise, they push and test our strength and resilience to the max. But, at least he was brave enough to share his problem and, by doing so, he had started out on that long road to recovery. Best of luck young man, you have a mature head on those shoulders

A couple of days later I left the hustle and bustle of Kota Kinabalu behind. Now travelling with a great Kiwi fella, Connor, who I'd also met in our hostel, we travelled down to Sepliok Orang-utan Rehabilitation Centre, which was home to Orang-utans, strangely enough. As I walked around, patiently waiting for the start of the visitors' circus trick - performing for the chimps at feeding time – I passed one of the centre's workers who was whistling the Scorpions' 'Wind of Change,' I suddenly glanced up and looked back. How strange? Could this be some kind of spiritual sign? Either way, I was recognising the need to keep focused on the upcoming issues in the UK to be sorted out and of course planning the Camino de Santiago too.

The decision to walk the Camino is one that seemed to get stronger every time I thought about it. One thing for sure is that I will walk it to raise money for Bury Hospice - and also for the memory of every person who has passed over with cancer. I feel now that I am on a mission to push, challenge and shape myself into the person I am supposed to be and in the direction I am supposed to be heading. If nothing else I feel confident that this year has been a springboard to new directions and to create lasting change. It has been a giant leap into the unknown and I have developed and grown so much as a person that change is now inevitable.

***

Moving on, we went on a great three day cruise on the

Kinabatangan River, spotting and snapping the delights of Borneo's diverse and marvellous wildlife. I enjoy connecting with nature; being surrounded by the animal kingdom gives me inner peace and, believe me, there is no finer place to do it than Borneo. There is so much to see here. Down by the river elephants crashed out of the jungle to the water's edge and ate leaves right in front of our speedboat. From the safety of the forest canopies, proboscis monkeys sat eating and staring inquisitively at the boat loads of travellers; various species of highly wondrous hornbills took off, soaring across the wide river; beautiful, brightly coloured kingfishers perched on branches looking for their next meal and, of course, there were the ubiquitous insects – lots of the bloody things.

Against this backdrop and a cacophony of jungle sounds, Connor and I chatted about our plans for the future, what we both wanted from life and how we'd hoped to fall in love again.

***

Things were becoming a little clearer by now. I'd done some networking and appointed an editor, I'd arranged for my house to be placed on the market and Bury Hospice had been in touch, so the Camino walk looked more likely to be cemented firmly in place. I also had a potential teaching job pencilled in for China should I wish to head down that route. So were things now moving forward? Are there potentially exciting times ahead? Is my rightful place in life one step closer? Hopefully the opportunities, strength, motivation and helping others will start to pay off.

***

After the river cruise, we headed off to the town of Sandakan which proved to be a poignant, but necessary, place to visit. It certainly made me reflect on how lucky I am. During the Second World War, this was the site of the infamous 'Death Marches.'

In 1945, this Prisoner Of War camp held over 2,400 allied troops, mainly from the UK and Australia, who were starved, beaten and tortured by their Japanese captors. In January 1945, the advancing allies bombed the military airstrip which the prisoners had been forced to build three years earlier. Fearing that the camp was about to be liberated, the camp commander ordered the camp to be moved immediately. In a series of marches between January and June 1945, the 1,900 POW's still alive were forced to move the camp to Ranau, a distance of 260km. Only 38 survivors made it to Ranau. Deemed unfit for any work, and many being too ill, they were shot by their captors, possibly after the war actually ended in August. In total, six Australian servicemen escaped and survived. I could feel the oppression hanging in the air like a thick carpet of pain wrapping itself around me as I walked around in disbelief.

This former POW camp is now a memorial garden and museum. Reading the inscriptions and information notices, it was extremely hard not to become emotional at what these men had endured. Beaten, shot, dying from dysentery or other awful diseases, these poor souls must have gone through sheer hell. As I drifted silently around the place, the oppression and negativity echoed through every last reminder to what once stood on the site - an unnecessary evil and one that should never have happened. There was sombreness to the place on a par with the killing fields of Cambodia. Here though, only a mere handful of people visited daily - hopefully not a place that any of them would forget. I certainly wouldn't.

Leaving Sandakan, we flew from Borneo into Kuala Lumpur for a couple of days before Connor and I parted company. He went west to Langkawi to meet up with Amy, a young girl from Jersey. Ironically, he had met her the day after we had chatted about falling in love. Staying in the same hostel as us in Sandakan, they had shared a connection and planned to meet up again. Strange isn't it, how sometimes these things happen quite by chance when we least expect them to? Once again proving the old phrase 'don't look for it, cos it will never come'.

And now perhaps, love had knocked on Connor's door...
I made my way on the overnight bus from Kuala Lumpur towards the Perhentian Islands on the east coast. Gazing out of the window up into the night sky, I suddenly had a thought; who would have thought that I, a man who had never written a thing in his life, could now write a book about his experiences, potentially opening up and creating a new future, all off the back of adversity? It made me think about who knows what any of us are really capable of, if only we could find the courage. Quite often, as in the books I'd read, these things seemed to come on the back of a trauma of some description. Admittedly, by comparison, my experiences had been nothing like theirs but they still provided an opportunity for me to make choices and take on new challenges.

With only three weeks remaining, accepting that this trip was nearly over, I once more had fears of returning to UK, the biggest one being returning to my old life. This is where determination and resilience really had to set in, making it totally clear there is to be no way back to a life that neither fulfils my needs nor inspires me.

Now, with the memories this year had brought, I understood more than ever the importance of having to live my life, not anyone else's. If something is destroying us, we have to find the courage not to follow the crowd or please others, even those that mean the most to us; we have to do what we feel is right for us.

A life full of regret is an unfulfilled life. With what had happened to people I knew whilst being away, I had become even more determined to live my life to its fullest extent. I had come to realise that breaking the chains that once bound had released untapped potential. I now needed to look upon using this trip as a platform or springboard to the life I, and indeed all of us, deserve to lead.

Once the shock of ten and a half months of travel is over, the focus shifts to planning the charity walk, selling the house and hopefully laying foundations for the future. At this stage it is clear that the Camino will be a great experience, and who knows what it may bring?

***

Connecting with a great bunch from the local dive shop, I had a great week on the beautiful and tranquil Besar, the largest of the Perhentian Islands, off the east coast of Malaysia, chilling out and diving. On a snorkelling trip I also had the opportunity to swim five metres down with the biggest green turtle I'd ever seen in my life - now that was breath-taking.

Reluctantly leaving the glorious and completely chilled out atmosphere of the Perhentian Islands behind, I'd decided to head north and back up into Thailand. There was nowhere left for me to visit in Malaysia really as I'd been here before, four years ago. Spending time on the islands of Ko Pha Ngan and Ko Tao seemed a far more attractive proposition, taking the opportunity to soak up any final bits of sun.

I left for the mainland on the 08.00hrs fast boat from the Perhentians, and the start of nearly 24 hours of travel. Jumping on a local bus to Kota Besur for the princely sum of 5RM, about £1, I changed buses and headed to the Malay/Thai border crossing, with Rantau Panjang on the Malay side and Sungai Golok on the Thai side. It suddenly occurred to me how life itself is like crossing borders as it can literally change from one thing to something completely different in a moment.

As I walked over the bridge into Thailand for the third time on this trip, I suddenly began to sing Iron Maiden's 'Brave New World' quite loudly and without my MP3 player plugged in either. Though I didn't quite manage to reach the vocal range of Bruce Dickinson, I nonetheless gave it a good go. Quite why that song came into my mind, I don't know; maybe it was because this was indeed like a brave new world, the anticipation of re-entering the UK, knowing that I would need every ounce of inner strength to keep going. It was up to me now to keep pushing forwards and stay focused.

After another five hour mini-van journey to Surat Thani, then taking the overnight ferry for seven hours, I arrived on Ko Tao, ready to relax and begin tying up loose ends for the last two weeks. First things first; I knew that just talking about walking the Camino could, in all honesty, turn into self doubt and procrastination once I'd arrived home. So, taking the elephant by the balls, I booked the flights for September and November so that there could be no doubt. Now it was set in stone and something positive to aim for and focus on.

The second thing I decided to do was the Advanced Open Water Diving course. I'd been a PADI Adventure diver since 2006 and, with thirty dives now under my belt, I decided to say stuff it and splash out the £80 or so to tie that one up. My Dive Master, Dennis and I swapped tales of travel and, being of similar age, shared the fact that we'd both reached points in our lives where unhappiness had forced change, reaffirming that only we can take personal responsibility to change what we don't want and focus on what we do.

Accepting an unexpected offer on the house back in England was the next loose end to be tied up. From out of the blue the tenants placed an offer and, even though I truly loved the house, neighbourhood and town, I had decided sometime ago that now would be the right time to sell. If I didn't, then I wouldn't be true to myself, would I? So what else could I do but accept their offer?

The next thing I began looking at was undertaking a CELTA certification which would help me become a better English teacher and give better job prospects abroad.

***

After five days on Ko Tao I decided to move on to the neighbouring island of Ko Pha Ngan. There I hired a moped and enjoyed zipping about, seeing what a lovely island this really is. Similar in size to Ko Lanta, it too had a relaxed vibe and feel to it. Ko Pha Ngan is home to the infamous Full Moon, Half Moon,

Black Moon and Jungle parties, where up to 30,000 drunken and high people turn up every month to party hard at the scruffy beach town of Haad Rin. For me though, silly parties weren't part of the agenda. I'm not some boring old fart but chilling, contemplating and maybe the odd yoga session were most definitely more appealing. Home to quite a busy ex-pat scene, the island has plenty to offer families and couples, as well as the party-goers.

Whist there, I'd heard about Pha Ngan Animal Care Centre, so I decided to pay a visit and see the work they did. After my month on Ko Lanta, I was keen to either volunteer or find out more about how the centre operates. Introducing myself to the manager, Laura, a lovely lass originally from Nottingham, she explained the work here and showed me the animal residents. Very similar to Lanta Animal Welfare, but on a much smaller scale, she talked me through her experiences and the stories of the various dogs here. It's always hard to hear stories of animal suffering; yet in some ways it is necessary, making the volunteer experience that much more powerful. As we talked, a black collie type dog was brought in to be treated. Someone, for a reason I will never understand, had cut off the little dog's left paw and a friction burn on his back looked like he had been dragged under a car too. The look of shock and sheer fright on his little face, combined with my own shock at seeing this, made me swallow hard. Who the fuck can do things like this to a defenceless animal? It beggars belief that a person can cut off an animal's paw just because it chases chickens. I was told that this barbaric act happens quite often in Thailand if an animal strays onto a farmer's land. As I gently held his head while we took his temperature, seeing his red and bloodied stump made my blood boil. Covered in lice, he was in another world, poor thing. Around the world the selfless work of treating these guys goes on at many centres similar to this one, often by low paid but dedicated and enthusiastic staff. It did resonate with me and I wished I had more time, not just on my trip, but on Ko Pha Ngan too. I donated £20 to a much needed fund, but wish I'd had more of an opportunity to help these poor animals than I did.

Chatting with Mario, a chap I'd met in a local bar, he told me that he'd lost his brother unexpectedly at the age of 42, dying suddenly at home in Dubai only a couple of weeks earlier. Still grieving and in shock, he was spending two weeks travelling, trying to reconnect with himself and come to terms with his loss. As I was nearing the same age as his brother it led me to reflect on my year. What a year. Not a single regret, only incredibly happy and fulfilling memories. It really has been one hell of a journey, one with twists and turns - and one with true purpose too. Yet it still resonated with me on how suddenly life can end, on how important it is to take opportunities to improve ourselves and enjoy life while we can - before it all comes to an end.

***

Flying is always an easier option than a sixteen hour bus/minivan/ferry journey. So, for the sake of £44, I took the ninety minute flight to Kuala Lumpur. With only three days before my flight to Manchester, lots of different emotions were going through my mind. On one hand, I was excited by the prospect of seeing family and friends, but on the other, with all the riches I had experienced, I knew it was going to be hard to leave Asia. The milk of human kindness and compassion has been amazing and I wanted to feel fulfilled in work/life, to continue helping people the best I can, inspiring others to help themselves. I think I have changed dramatically since 26th Sept 2011; I know I now have the walk to focus on, and no doubt will complete it, but it will be done with a purpose too, one that will hopefully touch people's hearts. It will certainly be a test to push boundaries and the limiting beliefs about what I am capable of. First and foremost I have to stay true to myself and then map out what I really need to do from then on. My mind is already made up, I will never return to the old way of living. I can adapt and cope with so much more. Living in huts and sheds had made me more resilient and capable of change.

Back in Kuala Lumpur, as I walked around the bustling, vibrant Chinese market, I thought back over the last eleven months. The people I'd met had been one of the highlights. I'd felt privileged to have met such inspirational ones, along with the many great travellers from all over the world; seeing up close how people pulled together to help each other. Never having witnessed adversity or felt threatened, I shall be sad to leave Asia again, but for now perhaps, I have too.

***

At 7.15pm on the 7th August, fifteen hours after boarding my flight on a hot Tuesday morning in Kuala Lumpur, I arrived at Terminal 1 in Manchester Airport. Once again, just like the time I was sitting on the boxes in my house in Harrogate, a strange sense of déjà vu washed over me. Spotting my brother patiently waiting for me, a sense of normality and familiarity also came over me. Giving each other a hug, the reality finally hit that my journey, well at least this part of it, was now officially over. It didn't seem fair actually, I hadn't wanted to throw in the towel, I'd wanted this journey, this wave of positivity, this new found confidence and belief in my abilities as a human being to continue. I wanted to carry on taking personal responsibility for myself, discovering how to live my life and not the one that I was expected to by those around me. For this year, I'd bloody well done that hadn't I?

Now though I had this strange mix of 'what ifs' and 'what now' relentlessly tapping on my mind. On both of the seven hour return flights I couldn't help but think - what happens now? After all, with the adventure I'd had, how the fuck would a normal, boring nine-to-five job ever be inviting again? Correct, it wouldn't. Never again, I'd told myself.

But, conscious that funds were drying up, issues had to be addressed, decisions had to be made. Well actually, long before

I'd smelled Manchester airport's tarmac, I'd started on that one. Firstly, the marital home that was now, to all intents and purposes, a shell of a house, had been sold without actually going on the market. First issue sorted. The second wasn't as easily solved though. If I was adamant that my former life was shed forever, what would I do about a job? Well, that was exactly what my dear old mother and father asked when I became reacquainted with them. The journey away taught me many things about my inner self, as you know. But I had learned much more than that about myself. I'd discovered that I could teach. By doing three voluntary stints as an English teacher, I'd uncovered a hidden talent; I could get my point across and, with more discipline and learning, I was sure I would make a highly effective teacher to foreign students. There was another hidden talent I'd uncovered too. If you have followed my journey this far you may have sussed what it is. Yes, I've discovered that I can write. If you remember, I felt compelled to put pen to paper after a shit time, even though I'd never written anything like it before. And yet, I've done it. I feel very proud of my journey, my trip and my achievements. In fact we all should be proud of what we uncover about ourselves as we walk the path of life. It is amazing, and this is how the beauty of life can reward us – by giving talents and new directions for us to follow, allowing us to develop even more as people.

So what's next for this intrepid traveller and adventurer? Yep, well guessed; another adventure.

After six days of desperately trying to adjust to life back in the UK, I was sitting in the office at Bury Hospice telling the fundraising manager, Michelle, all about my 'Boots, Beer and Bury Hospice' challenge. The Hospice had raised all but £500,000 of the £5 million needed for a new larger building. Perhaps this walk would go some way to help them reach their target, persuading people to part with their money for a very worthy cause. Let's hope so.

On leaving Bury Hospice, the mission was slightly clearer in my mind. Things seemed to be heading in right direction; the vision I'd had in Cambodia was starting to materialise. And who knows, maybe the walk will open some new doors?

But, just as today's positivity was cemented, so came the news that Pat, my next door neighbour, who was perfectly fine before I left the UK, would be moving into a Hospice in Yorkshire to see out her final weeks. About a month into my trip I'd received an email bringing the shit news that she had been diagnosed with cancer. Since that time she'd fought tooth and nail to defeat it, but now her cancer was no longer treatable. This again shows how important it is to live our lives as fully and as best we can. We never know what is around the corner.

Only a matter of days later, Pat, despite her brave fight, lost her battle, another victim to this bastard of a disease - further affirmation that the planned walk is important in so many ways. Let's hope it will raise awareness and resonate deep within those who read my sponsor page.

A week or so later I received a phone call from BBC Radio Manchester as they wanted an interview with me about my Boots, Beer and Bury Hospice fund-raising walk. All was going well and some three weeks later the house sale went through, finally sealing that memory for good. It was strange in a way; I felt sad about the house, with its memories and everything but sometimes things are just not to be. Besides, I had to let go of the past and embrace the future. At least the new owners are a lovely family and quite literally, the house has gone to a good home. The house had served its purpose for me, but at the end of the day it's only bricks and mortar. With it selling, it allowed me to buy an investment property and leave the path open to move forwards, to go abroad again.

The beginning of the week brought a photo shoot for the local paper, The Bury Times, with me holding a pair of walking boots in one hand and a pint of beer in the other. I almost felt like a celebrity, smiling for the camera. Knowing that I would be trying to achieve and accomplish another challenge - and for the benefit of so many other people too - gave me a warm glow. With the radio interview planned for the following Sunday, I remembered that I saw this happen in my mind's eye whilst travelling in New Zealand. That may seem weird, but, since the end of my marriage, everything that I had said I wanted to do, I have done - all ticked off and accomplished. I feel so proud of myself and now, on countdown to Camino I'm feeling much better, more positive about the future. With the doors from the past now firmly closed, I'm eagerly awaiting for new ones to swing open.

That week also brought the news that I had passed the interview for the CELTA course in Bangkok. Then, after finding the artist by chance, my ideas had now been transposed into the finished artwork for the book cover – a massive bonus. Later in the same week the interview and feature appeared in the Bury Times. It was quite good actually - although, so far, no sponsors have sprung from it. I felt a little let down, I'd tried hard with this, all with no previous fundraising experience to draw from. But you can't force people to part with money, especially as, at this time, most people in the world are skint and can little afford to fill the tins it seems that everybody is shaking at them.

Arriving at BBC Radio Manchester's studios at the ungodly hour of 06.45 for my interview on the 'Steve Saul' Sunday breakfast show, my nerves got the better of me until the interview started. Exchanging nervous chat with the show's producer, I remembered that I'd been on the radio once before.

"Aaah, that takes me back," I said as we left the lift and made our way to the comfy chairs and a much needed pot of coffee. "It was 1988 love, and the 'Gary Davies' show on Radio One. I'd appeared as part of the 'Unsung Heroes' feature – do you remember it?"

No, of course she didn't. It was twenty-four years ago and she was only about twenty years old.

Still, it was good. Alright, I sang like a twat, but it was fun.

Before I knew it, the signal came to enter the studio and await my cue. It went great, although I was slightly annoyed that my 'airtime' had been reduced to five minutes. But I did get some good feedback from friends who had listened in. I had hoped it would attract some more sponsors but it didn't. Sod it, I was doing my best and that is all that matters. As I write this, £420.00 is in the account. It doesn't sound much, but it's an achievement in itself. And with just three days before my departure to France, it is probably nothing to what I'm expecting the next six weeks of hard work to be like....

14
The Way of Saint James

Surprisingly, planning the Camino de Santiago did not take that much time. Once I had the sponsorship ball rolling, it was just a simple case of looking on various forums on the internet and tweaking travel plans and packing lists to suit. The medieval town of Saint Jean Pied de Port, close to the Spanish border, provided the starting point for the Camino that I'd chosen. There are twelve different ways, with five main Camino routes but, with around 150,000 pilgrims making their way over the Pyrenees each year, the 'Camino Frances' is the most popular way to get to Santiago de Compostela in Galicia, Northern Spain.

Even though I have made reference to the Camino de Santiago before, perhaps it is a good idea to explain its origins in a little more detail. Saint James was a disciple of Jesus and was beheaded by King Herod in AD44. His remains were thought to have been brought by his followers by boat from Jerusalem to Santiago where they are now preserved in a silver casket housed in its cathedral. Over the last 1000 years or so, various pilgrimages to visit his shrine have sprung up. St. Jean Pied de Port, a market town on a popular trading route at the foot of the Pyrenees, became a significant starting point for pilgrims. In French 'Pied de Port' literally means 'at the foot of the mountain pass.' Since around the 11th century, God knows how many pilgrims have walked from here-over the Pyrenees and on to the city of Santiago, 789.1 km away.

With the seed that Ross had planted firmly in my head around 10 months previously, I wanted to make sure that this experience would be a memorable one, so the process of planning and preparation had to be pretty damn good if I was to successfully walk the Camino in 30 to 35 days. Walking around 14-17 miles every day is no mean feat and packing a rucksack that you have to carry needs careful thought. If I carried too much it would hurt my back, my knees and, not forgetting the very things that would be carrying me to Santiago, my feet. After consulting the forums on numerous occasions, four words sprang to mind - pack light, pack right. I planned to pack my 35 litre rucksack with a meagre yet essential kit of waterproofs, jacket, 2 T shirts, 3 tech layers, 3 socks, 3 boxer shorts, 2 trousers, sandals, toiletries, towel, sleeping bag and liner, water platypus, hat, cap and gloves. Weighing in at around 8.4kgs, around 10% of my overall bodyweight would have to be carried on my back for nearly six weeks.

I was more than a little dismayed to discover that nearly all of the 5kgs I'd lost on my travels had been put back on in the six weeks since I'd returned to the UK. A combination of shitty processed foods and my own greed had resulted in a bloated stomach. Still, no doubt I'd be sweating madly in the coming weeks, so hopefully the weight would fall back off again.

The past few weeks had allowed me to train hard for what was coming. With well-worn boots, blisters shouldn't be a problem, although having to walk around 7-8 hours a day, every day, might be. Despite all this, I was now really looking forward to this walk. Walking is a big passion of mine but to do it continually for six weeks could potentially make me hate it from then on.

I felt a sense of pride in having raised nearly £450 for Bury Hospice, although I had a lot of help from the chaps at the fundraising department who assisted me in getting to grips with my social media campaign and twitter page.

As the day for leaving approached I again was squirming around with my comfort zone being squeezed madly. I'd never done any fundraising before and I would have to provide regular updates on my progress to encourage more sponsors to come in. Even so, I felt ready to tackle this fresh challenge with the vigour and anticipation that I'd become so used to over the past 18 months.

***

I'd often wondered why, in 42 years, I had never before set foot in France. Now, as my plane landed in Biarritz, I realised why. It was full of French people. Not that I have anything against them but the buggers won't speak English and I can't speak bloody French. At the airport I casually asked a simple question to a young lady sweeping up in a café. The look I was given was not unlike the one I would have received had I defecated in the poor lass's handbag. Unfortunately my knowledge of the French vocabulary was limited to that fondly remembered from my schooldays and the rather cute but totally pointless 'C'est Une Stylo,' - this is a pen - wasn't going to get me far. It certainly wasn't going to get me any cash or the directions to my pre-booked, overpriced motel for the night. So it was little wonder that, having walked round in bloody circles, it took me over an hour to travel the 800 metres from the airport to the hotel. And when I did finally arrive, the automated check in machine failed to recognise my booking. After frantically knocking on the door to wake the night porter, then performing a mime routine that would have scared children away, my point that I couldn't get into my fucking room was eventually recognised.

The next morning, after a dreadful continental breakfast of croissant and coffee whilst being stared at by middle class French people committing serious fashion violations and holding dogs in the next door cafe, I boarded the bus to Bayonne where I was to catch the train to St. Jean Pied de Port- the gateway to the Camino de Santiago.

As the train waited in the station I glanced around, noticing others patiently waiting to board. All were silent, busy gazing at the sky or the floor. I presumed they were pilgrims too as they all had that familiar look of trepidation, unsure of what to expect. As the train sounded its horn and pulled away on this sunny September morning, it reminded me of a trip to Hogwarts, with the old fashioned style carriages and everybody on the train there for the same reason. The hour and a half journey would get me in for around 1 o'clock, far too late to walk the first 27kms over the Pyrenees. By the time I arrived, the music of Metallica and Iron Maiden had fired me up no end and I was virtually buzzing as I made my way towards the Tourismo office to collect my pilgrim credential. This passport needs to be stamped every day, usually at the albergue's that pilgrims are allowed to stay at, so you can collect your Compostela or certificate of completion at Santiago, proof that you have indeed walked the full 789kms. After completing the registration and now officially a 'pilgrim,' I made my way to the albergue to drop my rucksack in. This would be the first of probably 30 or so I would have the pleasure of staying in over the next 5-6 weeks.

So, I hear you ask, what the bloody hell is an albergue? Basically, it's a cross between a dormitory full of beds and a youth hostel. All have a kitchen, showers and toilets and, for between 5-8 euros, they provide basic shelter and a bed. What else do you need other than a place to have a crap and a shower, and of course, to meet other pilgrims?

St Jean Pied de Port, a beautiful, historic, well preserved and authentic medieval city, reminded me so much of York in the UK. I spent most of the day walking around it, again realising my French was bloody crap. Looking at the menu, I ordered food without having a clue what I was ordering. Still, tomorrow, I'd be over the hill and into Spain, at least they'll speak the Queen's language. Won't they?

The rules of the albergue's stipulate no noise and lights out between 10 and 10.30pm. Bugger, I thought, how the hell will I sleep so early? In days to come, believe me, it would not be a problem. But on this, the eve of the first day's walk, my apprehension over what lay ahead made sleeping difficult.

Albergue's do not usually have separate male or female rooms, so it's common to see people of both sexes walking round in their underwear or sleeping attire. No problem with that at all - unless of course they are fat, miserable, female and German. Indeed, on that first welcoming night most of us were kept awake by the snoring of two large ladies from the aforementioned country, who did nothing but complain at every opportunity, had faces like a bulldog licking piss from a thistle and who snored relentlessly, making a sound like a heavy object being dragged across a wooden floor. Good job I'd packed earplugs because they would prove invaluable throughout this trip.

The next morning, just after 6am, the dorm lights came on. Then began the slow procession of 25 or so people moving about and packing rucksacks before sitting down for a communal breakfast which, feeling more like a condemned man's final meal before being taken outside and shot, formed a memorable reminder to my first stay in an albergue. It was a quiet affair, no-one quite knowing what to say, politely ignoring each other, silently drinking coffee out of a cereal bowl. With nerves giving way to anticipation of what lay ahead, you could have cut the atmosphere with a knife.

At around 7 o'clock on a dark Friday morning, I left the albergue and silently drifted down the hill, through the town and found the first marker of the trail, a scallop shell, pointing the way to Roncesvalles. Over the years there has been mythical, metaphorical and practical meanings to its significance, but the grooves of the scallop shell represent the various routes pilgrims travelled to Compostela and now it is traditional for modern day pilgrims to carry one with them as they walk this pilgrimage.

You could have heard a pin drop; there was not so much as a bird in song, just a dark eerie silence. Deafening. In the dark I walked along country lanes until I began to catch up with some other pilgrims. Luke was one, a young lad, bearing an uncanny resemblance to the tennis player, Andy Murray. An 18 year old American, he'd lost his father at 14 and was unsure of his future plans and hoping to find himself. He provided pleasant company as we walked in the breaking light of morning. I felt good and happy to be free once more to spread my wings whilst still doing some good for the world.

Throughout the morning, as the road ahead climbed higher, I swapped and shared pleasantries and stories with other pilgrims from around the globe. That first days 27 km hike was breath-taking and arduous, long enough to let your legs know they'd been busy and to introduce them to the fact that they would have to get used to it over the next 30 days or so. I'd been told to expect some difficult weather crossing the Pyrenees but it was a warm day with hardly a breeze, affording some truly stunning views across the mountains.

At around half past four, a weary band of pilgrims, having crossed the border into Spain, descended from the heights of the Pyrenees into Roncesvalles and into a stunning monastery, and to what can only be described as the Starship Enterprise of albergue's. It was bloody massive, and full of pilgrims.

Then began what was to become a daily ritual of shower, sock and underwear washing, write in journal, rest, read, listen to music perhaps; then several beers before bedtime.

That evening I sat in the restaurant for what would become the first of far too many 'Peregrinos menus' over the next month. Comprising of a choice of usually 4 or 5 starters, a choice of the same number of main courses, a sweet, bread, - or 'pan' as it's called here - water and the infamous 'Vino Tinto de la Casa'. That first bottle of house red wine shared between four of us went down quicker than a granny on black ice. I wasn't sure what I'd expected it to taste like but, with the Rioja region next door, it tasted far better than the 'Chateaux Shit-House' you would get for the same money or more back in the UK. And the princely sum for this feast, you ask? Why, between 8-11 euros, my friend. The ritual of the evening feast became a crucial part of the Camino experience, and climbing the ladder into my top bunk later in the evening, this pilgrim was pleasantly pissed with vino and the sheer adrenaline and fulfilment of completing that first day's hiking. Now, the next question–after 'how the fuck do I get down this bloody ladder quietly at 2 in the morning when I'm bursting for a piss' - was 'can my legs do it all again tomorrow, and would I get blisters for my efforts too?'

Around 6am, feeling the cold and with a head full of goon, I heard the first groans of 'it's pissing down' ringing through the long corridors of the dormitory. Everyone began leaping out of bed, enthusiastically stuffing their rucksacks and heading off into the first light of morning. It was indeed raining, and feeling rather gracious about packing the right wet weather gear, it soon became my turn to head off towards Larrasoana, some 27 kms in the distance. As I set off alone, a good feeling washed over me. I'd met some thoroughly nice people so far and all seemingly with something they wanted to solve or overcome in their lives. I'd shared my story of fundraising with some pilgrims and felt fortunate to have the time to reflect on my own pilgrimage. There was a long road ahead and it took some getting used to the idea of what walking this spiritual adventure would take, after all 789km is a long way.

I arrived into Larrasoana tired and hungry but with my feet surprisingly okay. Following the route map, the next day's romp would only be a short one - into the city of Pamplona, home to the festival of San Fermin, the highlight of which is the famous 'running of the bulls.' Here, what can be only described as 'pillocks' try, and fail miserably, to outrun several tons of stampeding prime beef let loose and trapped within the city's narrow cobbled streets. A city steeped in medieval history, I took the time to explore and sample the local 'pinchos' - known as 'tapas' in other parts of Spain. The albergue here, in keeping with the bovine theme, reminded me of something akin to a cattle market. It was large and did not really have enough facilities for the 150 or so bedding down every night. I enjoyed the giant youth hostel atmosphere but I was already tiring of the incessant snoring, burping, farting and belching erupting through the darkness- and that was just the ladies.

That evening I chatted with Andreas, a Danish chap who'd started to walk the gigantic Appalachian Trail in America the previous year but had to stop and return to his homeland after he'd received the sad news that his mother was dying from cancer. Now, feeling the need to walk the Camino in her memory, his core values of life had been stripped back to their basics. As people were now starting to open up and mix with other pilgrims, how many other stories would I hear like this over the forthcoming adventure? Quite a few, I expect, although the main topic of conversation that evening was whether or not our feet would hold up for another relentless barrage tomorrow.

I awoke the following morning to a new day and a new month. And what a beautiful day it was to hike out of Pamplona, pleasantly stuffed with wine and pinchos, ready to make the next assault towards Cizur Menor and the end of the first 73kms. As I set off I noticed something I found quite amusing. When passing familiar groups of walkers, it reminded me of the film 'The Cannonball Run.' Seeing team 'Spain' or 'Korea' or 'mom and daughter,' this looked like some sort of wacky race. That's part of the fun I guess, and hell, do you need to keep yourself amused walking for up to seven hours a day?

As day four ended in Puente La Reina with the first 100kms completed, I began noticing the number of people suffering with blisters or shin splints on the increase. Mind you, some of those were carrying backpacks like they were on some sort of trek to Kilimanjaro. You could almost feel their pain from the weight hanging off their shoulders. Just what the fuck had they brought? Carrying your house on your back for nearly six weeks is difficult to imagine, but common sense when filling it is much needed. It's hardly any kind of fashion parade, after all most of us pilgrims wore socks and crocs or sandals on an evening just to give the old feet a break. Very Germanic, I know, but an absolute necessity and everyone was guilty of committing serious fashion violations in the name of comfort.

As the days turned into the end of the first week, I was totally enjoying the sights and sounds of nature as I walked amidst this amazing scenery. As I made my way across Northern Spain, under a deeply intense blue sky, autumn painted its orange, brown and burnt ochre colours across the ploughed fields. As the hot burning sun beat down relentlessly on my face, it really was like walking into a postcard and I soaked it up like a sponge. As we descended into yet another deserted town or village, passing the obligatory tumbleweed as we walked down empty streets devoid of any sound, wondering whether we had walked into the film set of '28 Days Later,' I thought; why do these lazy bastards need an afternoon siesta? By now though I'd got used to the fact that everywhere would be shut, then re-open come 5 o'clock. That night over yet more Vino Tinto, tales were shared of one lad's mission to walk across America ending with a stress fracture after 260kms and another's tale of walking the Appalachian trail ending after personal problems. One had lost his father, the other his mother. I shook my head in admiration as they unburdened how they dealt with their devastating losses. I felt incredible lucky to be meeting such lovely and real people from around the world with maturity beyond their years, all being able to share their deepest and darkest fears in the company and comfort of strangers. Priceless.

Another highlight early on in that first week was to pass a fountain at Bodegas Irache, some 4kms into the days tramp, and help myself to a glass of red wine at 8.30 in the morning. I kid you not. There it was, a fountain offering free red wine - and as much as you could drink too. Not much use at that time of the morning, but it was bloody good. Imagine that in the UK? It wouldn't last two minutes before the 'Health and Safety' Nazis closed it down for being irresponsible or some other excuse. Still, it was another experience on the Camino enjoyed by many and it provided another good use for my scallop shell too.

The daily ritual was becoming clearer now– sometimes walk

on your own, sometimes with other people for a mile or two, then on your own again, listen to music or perhaps soak up the atmosphere of what this pilgrimage was becoming and the sheer joy of being able to do something like this and escape from the bustle of modern life. On a night, somewhere I'd find those I had connected with and catch up on the stories of the day. Passing through the many villages en route, it was not uncommon to find pilgrims stopping and entering some quite beautiful little churches, either to marvel at their intricate beauty or to offer prayers - myself included. At times it became a source of comfort.

The whole experience was starting to become a Camino family now. With smiles, greetings, waves and shoulders to offload onto, most pilgrims would offer help to each other as and when necessary and usually without expecting thanks. This was fast becoming a unity. And why not? After all, we all live under the same sun and walk under the same moon. By now, the familiar faces I walked with and passed by had turned into a motley crew on an evening. With Pat, Pete and myself from the UK, Jesper and Andreas from Denmark, Simon from Australia and Luke and Eric from the US, evenings had become quite fun, without detracting from the seriousness of why we were all walking during the daytime. By the time the next day got underway, attacking the long 30 km road from Los Arcos to the sprawling city of Logrono, I sat down outside a pavement cafe for the first coffee of the day. As I bent down to place my rucksack on the floor, a single white feather appeared. Seeing it as another spiritual sign, I carefully picked it up and attached it to my rucksack. My lucky charm, I believed - and it gave me strength that I must have needed. It had been a day of reflection and contemplation and that evening, sitting outside a bar in Logrono, I thought about the following day, where another 28km walk loomed; this time to Najera.

This was one that I attacked in almost total silence. By this time my feet were beginning to burn, feeling like they were on fire. It was touching 25 degrees nearly every day, and it was certainly tough going out in the heat of the Mediterranean sun. Nothing had prepared me for its relentless onslaught. Admittedly, it made the landscape shimmer in a golden glow, a just reward for walking up to 7 hours a day in its glory, but it sapped energy levels and made my feet swell more. Rather than complaining, I thought about the suffering of many people around the world, of what their pain must be like. It was like a metaphorical slap around the face, telling me not to complain but to 'man up.' It worked too.

Walking through the Basque region, I'd noticed that both the quite ridiculous 'mullet' and the 'Christmas jumper' figured highly on the 'fashion list' here. With all the talk about ETA terrorists, I figured that seeing this was far scarier than some knob with a gun. I had come here expecting to walk a long way but I hadn't expected to be walking back into the '80's. This thought made me smile and cheered me up.

Due to my fitness level I'd covered more than the recommended daily mileage so I had in fact made up a day. This was great, as there had been talk, even at this early stage, of extending the walk and covering a further 90kms to Finisterre, considered in medieval times to be the end of the world. This would be a nice extension if I decided the 789kms to Santiago hadn't been enough. It had seemed like a great idea as we chatted about it on that first crisp morning hiking out of St. Jean Pied de Port, but now it needed a good dose of 'mind-bleach' to erase the notion that walking any further than necessary in the name of fun was just fucking stupid. Walking every day was beginning to take its toll, but there was no way I was going to stop.

Checking in on emails that evening, there was one about teaching English in China. I don't want to pursue that one just yet, maybe see what else comes, but either way I'll have my investment flat in Harrogate to sort out on the return to the UK. Many of the pilgrims preferred to walk with others, some preferred to be on their own. Personally, I was equally comfortable either way. By now though, I was walking by myself. Being on my own meant that time was readily available to contemplate and reflect on life. One of the reasons this walk is so popular is that it offers the pilgrim the opportunity to really connect with themselves and clear away unwanted clutter from their lives. For me the uncertainty of the future meant there was always something to discuss with myself.

"Fuck it," I announced to the forest one morning, "Live for today, not tomorrow, for tomorrow may never come." I then thought back to a quote I'd come across the other day 'Yesterday is history; tomorrow is the future; today is a gift - that's why it's called the present'. How true that is. Pulling the waistband of my ever slackening trousers up off my arse, I marvelled in the beauty that surrounded me. Being able to connect with the universe, surrounded by nature, embracing it at its fullest was truly a gift. More than anything I loved breathing in the pure mountain air and hated every minute of passing through towns and cities with locals blasting the horns on their shit cars. I was certainly relishing this endurance feat, pushing and challenging myself each day, shifting my pain by thinking of those who don't have a choice, sending out healing thoughts whenever I could.

By the end of day 9, with a dull constant throb emitting from my feet, I reached the medieval town of Belorado. There, 3 Israelis unexpectedly stopped me in my albergue to invite me to join them to share the dinner they'd cooked, my first experience of the 'Power of the Camino.' That's what it became known as, when total strangers offered random acts of kindness to pilgrims. Why can't the world do this as a matter of course, I wondered? It would be a better place if we all could adopt this kindness.

Our little band of merry men had by now separated. We all walked at different speeds and paces, so we weren't always guaranteed to meet up at the end of the day. There was no shortage of albergues along the route and some preferred to stay at less crowded or private ones. So, for the next couple of days the unfamiliarity of not knowing anyone pushed me to mix with new and interesting pilgrims.

The walk into the city of Burgos, proved to be the shittest day so far. The last 10kms were totally on tarmac and by the time the giant municipal albergue appeared, my feet felt like they had been attacked with a bamboo cane. Burgos, with its imposing cathedral, narrow streets and medieval history would have been a great place to rest and sightsee for a day but I was keen to carry on walking. So I left the next morning, following the familiar yellow arrows painted on roads, trees or kerbs, pointing the way out of the city. By the end of the first 6kms, the rain had started and my left leg began throbbing uncomfortably like it was on fire, the first injury for me on the trail. Unable to carry on, a pilgrim stopped and checked if I was okay. The pain subsided with some anti-inflammatory, and I continued past my original 20kms destination for a further 11kms, past an intended halfway albergue that was shut, before finally hobbling into the quaint village of Hornillos, my feet badly swollen and in total agony.

The next morning, as I slowly hobbled the 10kms into Castrojeriz, I remembered that the Camino is split into 3 stages. The first stage is physical as it is tough and hard; the second is mental as it is flat, fairly uninteresting and with long stages of nothing; then the final third being spiritual, with time for reflection as you descend into the finish of Santiago. I was now on the verge of ending the first stage and entering the second. I was not only truly enjoying the unique experience of what the Camino had to offer, I was also hoping to discover more about myself as the days passed by.

After taking a much needed break for the day at Castrojeriz, the following day I collapsed in sheer agony after just 15kms, with what felt like hot daggers being twisted into my left leg. The pain was so bad I went down quicker than a $10 whore. Diagnosing my problem as shin splints, I just couldn't go on. But then, from out of nowhere, the Power of the Camino kicked in. One pilgrim passing gave me high dose Ibuprofen and another gave me his walking stick. Then, as I massaged my swollen leg, an Aussie fella offered to carry my pack for 3 kms and two Irish lasses gave me a support bandage. Having this sort of help felt great and very humbling, help you can call on without asking. That is what happens on the Camino. If you can help someone out, you do - no questions. How powerful is that?

In Boadilla, after cutting the days planned walk short, I unexpectedly caught up with some of the merry men once again, so we took the opportunity that night to empty a few more bottles. The following day I headed out on a quite stunning, fresh morning, walking alongside a canal path offering quite breath-taking photo opportunities of the mist gently rolling away from the landscape. It was here I discovered a cat that was fitting. Clearly in distress, I gently padded its head, moved him onto the grass and stayed with him until he came out of it. In Spain there are literally hundreds of stray cats and this was just one, but there was no way I could see him suffer. Moving on, the leg was holding up, but it was the heavy riffs of Slash that carried me onwards towards my bed for the night.

Over the next couple of days, the weather turned cold and blowy and the landscape became boring with nothing to see or to stop and look at. With my pack heavy with extra food and water, it made me think about the rucksack of life that we all carry on our backs, filled with our experiences. Every so often it becomes so full that we must empty it before new experiences can fit in. For myself and many others this was what the Camino was partly about; truly letting go of burdens and clearing room for exciting new opportunities ahead. Perhaps that is why it felt lighter by the time I got to Mansilla. Unfortunately, by the time Leon came into view the following day, with the 18 kms covered in wet, miserable, shitty conditions, another kilo or two seemed to have been added to the pack. I had hoped to have met someone nice again, but I haven't and that was one thought constantly going around my head - but a pilgrimage is a pilgrimage and each one is a penitence to reflect on oneself and on the suffering of others. With my walk being for charity, I am constantly reminded about that. You learn a lot about yourself walking like this, how to interact with others better and to think of how to heal our wounds. I'd love to know the answers to some of my own questions about life, but how do I start to unravel that? Being alone with just your soul and your thoughts for company can be a start, but what a true joy to be able to put this experience into your own rucksack of life, eh?

Leon has to be one of the highlights, city wise, on the whole Camino route. A vast, sprawling city steeped in history and with an incredible gothic cathedral, providing an impressive backdrop to exploring this medieval wonderland. In fact, many pilgrims choose to make this their rest day, to spend it sightseeing and taking a well- earned breather. Having arrived on one of the wettest days of the whole walk, I chose not to - although I did take time to explore the cathedral. I stayed in an ancient albergue complete with an evening pilgrims' mass in the church next door. Neither being Catholic nor speaking a word of Spanish, I, along with 20 or so other worldwide pilgrims, sat miming the words and staring at the vast array of nuns who appeared almost pantomime like from a side door, yet proceeded to sing quite beautifully whilst being conducted by an elderly nun. What a quite nice experience to have. It brought people together and a warm glow to a cold wet evening. It didn't cost anything either.

The next morning, I slipped out into heavy rain and left the concrete jungle of the suburbs behind. I was glad to be away. For me, and many others, the Camino isn't about visiting big cities. They are wondrous nonetheless and a necessary part of the whole route.

I was now tiring of the 'cattle market' albergues, where as many pilgrims as possible are herded in like cattle with little privacy and insufficient bathroom facilities. I'd enjoyed them, as they always meant meeting the familiar faces of other pilgrims but I was looking for something different now, and not the dreaded bed-bugs either. These horrible little critters had been mentioned by many and caught by some unfortunate to have crossed their path. Fortunately, I'd not met their acquaintance, but saw the vicious red marks they'd inflicted on some poor sleeping pilgrims. It almost became like playing Russian roulette whether you'd end up catching them or not. It didn't seem to matter whether the place was clean either. The only thing you could do was cross your fingers and look carefully at the beds before you unravelled your sleeping bag. If you did catch them you had to either wash everything at high temperature or stick your sleeping bag in a freezer.

My leg felt healed now and yet I felt morose as I trudged through two solid days of wet. There were only 12 or 13 days left now and I had really enjoyed every minute of it so far. That evening in a smaller, compact albergue, complete with bar, I connected with Linn, a lovely little Norwegian lass who shared an all too familiar tale. After splits with partners she'd become unsure of her life's direction; she'd travelled and taken mundane jobs over the years that neither inspired nor motivated her. As a result she suffered from a lack of self-confidence. I understood that fully and, by the end of the evening, I'd tried to help as best I could, encouraging her to see further forwards than she was currently able to. Once again the Camino allowed people to connect and unburden, without fear of being judged or ridiculed.

Leaving the village of Villar de Mazarife, the sun shone brightly through this beautiful, clear, crisp morning. The path scythed its way through the golden yellow cornfield, revealing the mountains in the distance where we'd all be heading in the next couple of days. After the recent bad weather, to walk once more in the golden glow of autumn felt like a gift from above. The town of Astorga was reached and there I decided to take a much needed day off, catch up on sleep and chill out. 22 days of solid walking and a beard to match - I needed to sort that out too.

After 2 nights, batteries recharged and leg fully healed, I was back on the road again and heading 26kms towards Foncebadon. This was another warm day in paradise and, as I walked that morning across the stunning landscape somewhere between Santa Catalina de Somoza and El Ganzo, Gary Barlow sang loudly into my ears, reminding me that it really was a 'Beautiful World.' To celebrate that fact, I did the rucksack dance. I must have looked a right twat to anyone watching but hey, who cares? Not me. The more this experience of being able to step off the world and to live an authentic and simplistic life, the more I felt pulled towards it. Life is complicated enough, attracting clutter to it like a magnet; so if the chance to lead an alternative life comes up, can that really be a bad thing? I remembered what a good friend had asked me shortly before heading off for this charity walk: - 'Do you not think that you need to take responsibility instead of fucking off travelling?' What!? Just what the bloody hell did he think I was doing? Responsibility begins and ends with personal responsibility and I held that in abundance.

After a wonderful night in a small, rustic, warm and friendly albergue, I left the mountain village retreat of Foncebadon early in the morning. It was still dark and I admired the colours cast by the lightening sky and the warm breeze blowing across the path. The sun was up in its full mid-morning glory and the forest jumped alive with rich green foliage by the time I reached the iron cross at La Cruz de Ferro. Here, the tradition is to leave a stone that you brought with you at the beginning of your journey, say a prayer of thanks for a safe passage so far and ask for a blessing for the remainder of the Camino. The stone represents a burden, rather like the rucksack analogy before. Leaving a stone symbolises a burden left behind, leaving you to move on with your life. I approached the cross festooned with the scarves, stones, flags and many other objects that had been left by thousands of pilgrims, all shedding their burdens. I wrote a note, too personal to share I'm afraid, folded it and climbed the screed to the base of the cross and placed it on the shrine. The sun was strong and I sat outside a small church near the cross, bathing in its warm glow, breathing in its deep rays, meditating for what seemed like an age before continuing down the path. It felt good to spiritually cleanse myself and as I walked away, I marked the date as being the day I left everything behind and fully moved on to embrace whatever would be put in my life ahead. No more tears or anger, this was it. I wasn't sure what it may bring but at that particular moment- I didn't care. Rather like Christmas day in Vang Vieng - I didn't give a fuck; life would present itself when it needed to. My rucksack somehow felt like it contained feathers as I continued my journey along the path hugging the road, through lush green valleys with wind farms in the distance, the still autumn sky rendering them temporarily redundant. With the silent trickles from mountain springs and warm glows radiating from the faces of unburdened pilgrims I passed on the way, I felt a sense of being at one with nature and the universe as a whole. It almost felt like I'd stepped out of the world and entered a parallel universe of love, humanity and compassion. Such is the driving force accompanying the Camino.

After my clear-out at the cross, I felt ready to move on and stamp Monday 22nd October firmly into my mind as the day my life was to begin again. The next day marked the 25th walking day and I started off by leaving with Marina, a lovely Brazilian girl. I had to remind myself once again how lucky we were to have weather like this, it was stunning. Walking outdoors made me so appreciative of the fact I was alive and able to enjoy this privilege. The walking and the heat were starting to catch up with me though and I stopped 6kms short of my intended destination of Villafranca, staying instead in the tiny hamlet of Pieros. There were only 5 pilgrims there and it allowed me to have some intellectual and heartfelt conversation with Elsebeth and Jonathan. Together we put the world to rights over a superb vegetarian feast. It was such an intimate yet humbling experience, truly allowing strangers from all over the world to roll out the carpet of human kindness and share our life's journeys.

By the next day, a late start and foul weather had soured the taste of the previous night's jollity. Heading high from

Villafranca over the Pradela route, it was a case of head down and walk, eventually bringing me into Ruitelan and a Buddhist albergue. More surprisingly, it was like a reunion of every familiar face I'd met and connected with over the past three weeks. That night, over a fantastic meal, plenty of vino and excellent company in this compact home of love, 36 people from all over the world shared conversations and sang songs, accompanied by an Irishman playing the guitar.

The following day would bring us into O'Cebreiro in the county of Galicia and very close to the final 100kms of the journey. As you can imagine, there was a whole lot of mixed emotions, not just in my head, but in so many other people's too. We were almost praying not to arrive in Santiago as it would mean that this life enriching experience would sadly come to an end. The weather was colder here but the scenery was still stunning and I now began to savour every step, every view, every lungful of fresh, mountain air with the kind of attention you would lavish upon appreciating a good wine. My senses felt heightened, probably because I too knew that this part of my journey would shortly be confined to the banks of my memory. I'd been doing a video diary for my social media page along the way, allowing supporters to follow the proceedings. That was hugely enjoyable too and I loved playing the 'TV' presenter, giving me something else new to have a go at. I was quite proud of the achievements of the walk; by this time I'd raised nearly £600 and it seemed to be impacting and resonating with people back home. I'd been in some pain with my feet, but that pain was nothing compared to those who are ill and incapable of a walk like this, and that was always in my mind if I ever thought about complaining about it.

We were well into the 'spiritual third' now, and all kinds of thoughts raced around in my head. What had I learned about myself? That was one thought; not just about the walk, but across the last 12 months. I'd realised so much within that time, that only I could be the person to change the course of my future, the only person to take control and the only one to blame if things turned to shit.

Walking through the stunning, green valleys of Galicia reminded me so much of the Yorkshire Dales, or the Cotswolds even. And the weather was holding out too. Not long left now, only 6 days till Santiago. That night became one of the worst for sleeping. I was physically shattered but with the end looming, I found sleep hard to come by. I'd thoroughly loved and enjoyed every minute on this challenge and didn't want it to end. I'd stepped into a place of love, serenity, peace and compassion. Other pilgrims shared this, yet some wondered what they would do at the end; the walk had refreshed them spiritually yet it hadn't quite answered the questions they'd asked.

"The Camino," Lisa said the next morning, "Is like life. The beginning is hard, the middle boring, and the end like dying." It did seem like that. Then she shared her story of kindness on the Camino and it nearly had me in tears. She told me how she was crying by the side of the road after only 4 days as her painfully inadequate footwear had begun to destroy her feet. Often, as they say in life, coincidences happen and the 'Power of the Camino' was about to wrap itself around another pilgrim. As Lisa sat sobbing by the side of the road, a man appeared, walking his dog. Seeing her in distress, he asked if she was okay. Introducing himself as a doctor, he took her to his home and, whilst his wife made coffee, this modern day saint tended her blistered feet before offering to drive her the 20kms or so to the town of Estelle. Now, her story of good deeds doesn't end there. If you thought that kindness ended with a lift, you'd be wrong; it didn't. On the way to Estelle he took a detour. No, it wasn't to take Lisa to a nearby wood and take advantage of her - but to an outdoor shop where he bought her a 70 euro pair of walking boots. This was kindness unrivalled, and all this Good Samaritan wanted in return was for her to email him as and when she reached Santiago. Does that one act not show us how we are all capable of interacting with each other? Unfortunately, the world has, by and large, lost these humanitarian principles - but here, in the shelter of this thousand year old Catholic pilgrimage, values that form the basis of every religion in the world reign strong. It resonated deeply when she told me her story.

As I left Lisa after a couple of miles, I continued along the track. Thinking back to the start of the day, I'd begun in such a foul mood. I now understood why. I was shedding my skin, bringing things and experiences from my sub-conscious into the conscious and now I was realising that was why anger and frustration were washing over me. Since the iron cross I was determined not to allow these negative emotions to wash over me, yet this morning they had. Could this truly be the Camino helping me to flush out these mental toxins?

That evening, as I ate dinner in the small albergue I was sharing with only six others close to the town of Portomarin, Merv the host asked me:-

"What would be your best way of summing up the Camino?"

"A privilege," I replied. "A sheer and utter privilege." That is what this journey has been. How else can you describe the feeling of being free to walk amongst stunning scenery for thirty-odd days surrounded by so much love and peace?

As the finish line loomed, so did the thought of what would happen when I returned to the UK. Where would I go from here? With the last day's walk into Santiago looming, these thoughts whizzed around causing that familiar wave of trepidation to wash over me once more. 'Why does life have to be so complicated,' I thought; 'will a door swing open or do I accept defeat and head back to an office again?'

'Like fuck, I will,' came the answer from my subconscious, which also reminded me of the last 12 months and everything marvellous I'd accomplished. 'Never again' it screamed at me from within my forehead. Okay, my answer wasn't clear but I wasn't going to give up now. Why should I?

Two days later, as I walked with Jonathan, we reflected on our journeys.

"Allow things to happen naturally, be comfortable from within, know yourself and doors will open," he had said.

"I know I shouldn't focus on the 'finding a solution' bit; a square peg in a round hole never fits. Was that what I was trying to do?" I asked.

"If it is, then happiness can never come; be true to yourself; do all you can and who knows? But love yourself and embrace your current situation as a gift."

It made sense and, as Jonathan had been on enough journeys throughout his life, it resonated more. After we parted, I stopped and thought about what he'd said. As I did, I stopped worrying and relaxed, knowing that somehow my needs would be met and it would all work out in the end.

The penultimate day was certainly a 'bitter sweet' moment, in more ways than one. Not only was the Camino coming to an end, I also found out that the investment property I'd hoped to buy prior to leaving England had fallen through because the seller had suddenly decided he no longer wanted to sell it. Knowing this would mean that I would lose £500 didn't make me full of the joys of spring. Quite the opposite in fact, it helped to give the day a sour taste.

The final day started brightly enough. Ignoring the hordes of weekend pilgrims who'd turned up 4 days earlier in Sarria to walk the last 115kms; it was a case of heads down, soak up the last bastions of the atmosphere and drag your heels like fuck walking those final 18kms towards the final destination, and the end of a magnificent 33 days walking. As with most pilgrims, it was a bitter sweet moment. No one wanted it to end, but reality told us all that it had to. Emotions ran high that day, the sense of achievement and purpose brought a lump to the throat of many a pilgrim. For me, the fact that I'd accomplished yet another tick off the 'fuck it list' and raised money for charity made my chest swell with pride. Yet, by the time of around 2 o'clock in the afternoon, I could barely drag my feet any further as I finally reached the magnificent cathedral of Santiago de Compostela. Finding the pilgrim office around the corner and joining the large queue, a lump appeared in my throat as I handed over my credential, proudly showing the young lady my stamp from St. Jean Pied de Port as my starting point. I duly received my Compostela, acknowledging my achievement in completing nearly 800kms of walking. It was such a mixed bag of emotions and I tried to compose myself as every thought, emotion, person I'd met, and act of kindness I'd experienced over the past 5 weeks replayed through my mind like watching a film on fast forward. I needed to be alone, to gather myself before wanting to grab a beer and get as pissed as a rat, but everywhere I looked, familiar faces smiled and greeted me, proudly clutching their Compostela's too. Tonight indeed would be a celebration, and one that every pilgrim who'd walked the Camino de Santiago would savour during every remaining minute of their respective journeys.

For me, the journey didn't end. After 2 nights in Santiago and watching the Pilgrims Mass on All Saints Day in the cathedral, marvelling in the splendour of the swinging of incense in the huge metal container known as a Botafumeiro, the desire to walk again proved too much. I pulled my walking boots back onto my tired and swollen feet, did a video diary for Boots, Beer and Bury Hospice and walked another 90kms over 3 days to Finisterre. I just didn't want the journey to end, I wanted to milk every last drop available out of this magnificent experience whilst I was able to.

Was it worth it you ask? Yes of course it was, that 86.5kms was an achievement in itself, but there wasn't that many pilgrims and, aside from walking with a couple of great people I'd met previously, the biggest highlight was probably walking on the second day with a Danish woman who could have made a whore blush with her colourful yet entertaining language. Finisterre itself was a bit of an anti-climax compared to the splendour of Santiago. As I wandered around this historic Spanish city on the morning of my flight back to the UK, this time there were no familiar faces, no pilgrims excitedly greeting each other outside the cathedral. There was just me, my memories and reflections of what had once again been a fantastic journey. I had admitted that for now, this bubble had burst and another chapter of the journey had closed. Even more significantly, the walk symbolised the conclusion of a fantastic year of my life, a year in which I'd achieved so much personally and one that had so much purpose for other people too, culminating in fundraising for my local charity.

Now, that did bring a lump to my throat and a tear to my eye.

15
I Did It My Way

You know, I bet as you're reading this, the thought is probably crossing your mind as to whether or not there is a happy ending to this journey. At many stages as I wrote this book, as I explored not only the world, but also myself, I too thought about that. I had hoped there would be. Indeed, I thought that I probably deserved one.

I now realise that it was very churlish of me to expect a happy ending. Over the last year or so, one of the lessons I've learnt is that, no matter how hard we look, sometimes the doors we so desperately want to open quite simply won't until they are ready to, and no amount of getting angry or being pissed off about it can change it one bit.

The thing to remember here is that this is a real story written by a very real and genuine man. When I started writing this book, my sole intention was not to become a rich, successful author, but to help other people in so many different ways. Every word is honest, truthful, and meaningful- and, perhaps more importantly, has come from within. That alone does not give it the right to have a happy ending - a reality that was pointed out to me on the Camino de Santiago. However, I now realise that there is no 'happy ending' in the traditional sense - because this is not the end, it is just the beginning.

When I arrived back in the UK after my marathon walk, more questions echoed through my mind; what now, what next, what in the future?

Hold on, take a deep breath, and think about what has been

achieved since November 2010, just two short years ago. There have been so many things I've achieved and accomplished, so many problems faced and overcome. I believe that whatever I wanted to do differently with my life, I could - and in a truly amazing way too. I unlocked the shackles of a former life that suffocated my creativity and sent myself off on a journey, one heck of a journey mind, one where I pushed myself, and went fearlessly headlong into the unknown, bathing in the warm glow of new experiences, relishing each new challenge and adventure that appeared in my path. Rather than denying myself the opportunity by thinking what would perhaps happen if I didn't do something, instead I focused on what positives I could take to help myself, and to benefit the lives of so many others too, if I did do something.

Looking back over this journey there have been far, far too many positives to list and each one remembered makes the chest swell and the eyes moisten with pride, pride in accomplishing and overcoming many things I never thought I could.

And to think, if I had never decided to take that first 'risk' of going to Nepal....

Sometimes we need to remember that life isn't a dress rehearsal, there's no second chance. Nor is there a way to jump into a DeLorean, put time into reverse and live our lives in the past. We all have to accept ourselves as people and be comfortable in our own skin. Sometimes, as they say, 'shit happens.' And it does, but maybe from that adversity or negativity, we can turn it into something that outweighs its former self. We are far stronger and more resilient than we realise. I have learnt to expect nothing and to value and appreciate everything. I've learnt the true meaning of what we are, of all we have and how it can be taken from us at any time. I've learnt not to waste a moment of this precious gift called life and continue to strive to see more, do more, and be more. A life of regret is a life not lived. I suppose at least I won't fit into that box.

Having said that, I do have one regret, – at the age of 42, I have never been a father. However, it is what I have to accept, although I still tell myself that maybe that box will be ticked 'achieved' someday. Or maybe it won't. Either way, I understand that life still has to be lived in the best way possible and, make no mistakes about it, I have done that and will continue to try and do so. We all can, if that is what we choose. It is up to the individual to decide what is best for them.

So what next then, Phil?

Plenty. Almost as soon as I landed back in the UK things started moving again. Firstly, after losing the house I intended to buy in Harrogate, an even better one appeared from out of nowhere and landed in my lap. I asked for that on the final day of the Camino and it looks like that prayer has been answered. And, as you'll now know, I finished the book that I said I would write. I feel more driven than before, refusing to accept anything that's not right in my life, determined to do my best and move forwards. I certainly won't be returning to my previous job under any circumstances, despite pressure from some people. I'm worth so much more to myself than that. Being true to oneself is one of the hardest things to accept. It is too easy to waiver your identity in favour of pleasing other people rather than being true to who you are as an individual, standing on your own two feet and saying 'fuck off, I'll live my life how I want.' As I sift through the rubble from the past two years, I realise that I need to be outdoors, up a mountain perhaps, surrounded by the beauty of nature. I can't settle into suburbia anymore; I don't watch television or read newspapers, I haven't done since the day I left England. I know I love people and enjoy helping others; so maybe I need to look for appropriate volunteer possibilities that might uncover new opportunities? Who knows what may present itself? I don't know, but I do know I love being free. I've also learnt that if we always do what we've always done then we'll never know what we never knew. Whatever happens, I'm going forward with every new step into an unpredictable future. Don't forget, we might be dead tomorrow. Say bollocks to making plans and live every day like it might be your last. I don't want to be the richest man in the graveyard; there are no pockets in shrouds or tow bars on coffins. I never intend to fill my life full of meaningless clutter ever again; besides, it took fucking ages to clear the last bloody lot out.

As I'm being true to myself, of course I'm disappointed that certain girls in Thailand or on the Camino didn't think as I did, but then, I may have tried too hard for things to fit together. My answers are – as they are for all of us - inside; but maybe I'd been asking the wrong questions, or maybe it needs a different way of unlocking the door? What I do know is that I want to keep pushing, challenging myself even further, see what is next, and who knows what may happen? We are all responsible for ourselves and the pathways we take in life, and sometimes comfort zones are there to be broken out of so that we can create new choices, accept challenge's and make changes. I did that, I pushed myself to the extreme and, even though I'm not sure what is next, I can hold my head up high and enjoy life. At this moment in time my needs are met, so I can continue to help other people. In fact, I'm almost certain of that, although I've now got a house to renovate first.

In the last two years I have visited 13 countries, undertaken 9 charity and volunteer projects and raised £666.50 for Bury Hospice. What a list of achievements to put on my life's CV, and damn right, I'm proud of it. Oh, I almost forgot- probably one of the biggest achievements has been to write a book. I imagine that, had someone said all this to me 2 years ago, I'm sure I'd have told them to fuck off.

In fact, I remember that cold, dark, miserable Tuesday night in November 2 years ago, 2 days after my wife had told me our marriage was over. I was crying uncontrollably, sobbing into the pillow, thinking that my life was over, when suddenly the door to the spare bedroom opened and she walked in, sat on the edge of the bed, put her hand on my back and said:-

'I know it hurts, and I don't want to hurt you, but one day

you'll thank me for this, I'm doing us both a favour.'

I recall lifting my head up, turning around and saying that she had just ripped the heart out of my chest; how could I ever get over that? But sat here now, as I think back to that day, I know she was right. I'll never, ever forget those words. Thinking about everything I've ticked off, accomplished and achieved from that moment on, I want to thank her. In fact, I'm sure I've still got her number somewhere.....

Live your life, love your life and above all remember one simple thing -

Fucking well enjoy it!

God Bless x

About the Author

Phil Beswick was born in Bury, Lancashire in 1970. After leaving school he trained and worked firstly as a Graphic Artist, then as a Carpenter and Joiner. After joining the Civil Service in 1995, he moved to Harrogate, North Yorkshire and remained there until September 2011.

Through his career within the Prison Service he amassed experience in Counselling and qualified as a Life Coach in 2010 whilst developing into an effective and motivational manager. Over the years he has travelled extensively, volunteered with the National Trust as a Working Holidays Leader and as a gardener, then more recently as a Pets as Therapy volunteer.

In his spare time Phil is a keen cyclist and hiker. He has played guitar in bands in both Lancashire and Yorkshire. He built his own electric guitar in 1998 and still likes to pose in front of the bedroom mirror on the odd occasion. He is a PADI Advanced Diver and has dived all around the world.

He has recently returned to live in Bury and, as a keen Bury FC supporter, he can often be found in the Main Stand, shouting abuse at the referee.

Phil's philosophy on life is simple; try your best, do your best, be your best and, perhaps far more importantly, don't waste a minute of the life you have been blessed with. Expect nothing, and value and appreciate everything.

If you'd like any further information or to simply contact the author, please contact:
www.philbeswick.com or email phil@philbeswick.com

Up The Shakers!

3184175R00113

Printed in Great Britain
by Amazon.co.uk, Ltd.,
Marston Gate.